Monadnock Journal

MONADNOCK JOURNAL

RICHARD F. MERRIFIELD

DRAWING BY NORA S. UNWIN

The Countryman Press

TAFTSVILLE · VERMONT

These essays first appeared in *The Keene* (N.H.) *Sentinel.*
Permission to reprint them is gratefully acknowledged.

Library of Congress Cataloging in Publication Data

Merrifield, Richard.
  Monadnock journal.

I. Title.
AC8.M463   081   75-4677
ISBN 0–914378–09–0

Printed in the United States of America by
The Stinehour Press, Lunenburg, Vermont

TO MY WIFE

Janet Appleton Merrifield

Someone down the generations, on a rainy day perhaps, may discover musty cartons crammed with my journals, in the attic above the kitchen ell. Dear One of the future, judge me gently in the half hour of your perusal before you return downstairs to your more pressing life. You won't hear me, but I may be whispering thanks for your brief visit, and bending toward you with a smile of love for having made me feel, for a bit, a little less lonely up there. R. F. M.

WINTER

December

We are each of us the stuff of future legend. An ancestress of mine was supposed, while rocking a cradle with one foot, never to have ceased while she stealthily grasped an axe and split the skull of a foe who was pushing up a board in a cabin floor. I don't believe it, but it made a grisly bedtime story to the ghoulish delight of my generation. There are no such exploits in my own life, but any hint surviving me may spin me into legend. Merely the fact that I write before sunrise, pipe in teeth, coffee mug nearby, may make of me a mythic figure of Herculean industry and fixed purpose, whereas in truth I am still half asleep, my brain as vague as that of a wandering sheep.

The harps of Sumeria, the pipes of Greece hang silent in museums. We do not know what music they played. We do know, as music came later to be written. I am hearing fourteenth-century music composed by the blind Landini, son of the sculptor Jacopo della Quercia. Mercifully, I cannot hear the clash of arms in the Hundred Years' War of that time, or the battles of Crécy and Poitiers, the agonies of the Black Death.

I find hope in reflecting that it is the music, not the clash and cries, that survives, and that other surviving things are the works of Petrarch, Chaucer, Dante and the paintings of Giotto.

In a restaurant affrighted ladies report a green monster on their corner window. The restaurateur with casual bravado picks it off by its back. It is indeed a terror to creatures of its own scale, a terrible female who even devours her bridegroom the morning after. But as the ladies are told its name they plead, "Don't boil it!—along with the lobsters." All in the restaurant join the plea, as it gets around that it is a garden friend, a sentinel against pests —a praying mantis.

✠

We bring from the seacoast three small clamshells, bought at a gift shop. They are shut, emptied of life. Into their homes ingenious bipeds called people have inserted paper which expands into "blossoms" in a water glass. Well, if you are going to devour a soft shell clam it is a sentimental touch to place in its tomb a memorial bouquet.

✠

Armies of bacteria war over grains of soil. Are we so regarded by a distant Observer?

✠

There is magic in the commonest object. One needs only the patience and time to investigate it, whereupon the dustiest weed, the brown fallen leaf, a bit of rock, or what you will, becomes a major oracle, a talisman admitting one to the deepest questions and possibilities of the earth.

✠

Had I been longer in his algebra class I might have done better with that mixture of numbers and lower case letters. His name

4

was Berry, and he resembled one—short, plump, round and pink of face, with bright eyes and a cheery smile. I liked his short white beard and the happy flourish of his pointer, as if it were a baton and algebra a symphony. I moved away before I could discover the mathematical music he was experiencing as, gazing with delight at his equations on the blackboard, he joyfully invited us all to relish with him his beloved world of unknown quantities.

✥

I am reading four books. One is about mythology, one about music, another on insects, the fourth my perennial rereading of Marcel Proust's *Remembrance of Things Past*. I am wondering how they link up in my current thoughts. Perhaps gods, song, bees and recollection are not so remote from one another after all.

Take insects: Some have dances of communication to tell others where the nectar is. Only the other day a brave cricket, somewhere in my cellar, sang his little chirp. With demonic memory, pests return to our white roses every year. And if insects have no gods they may well be content not to be troubled with that unending human quest.

✥

A female kitten now lives with us. She is as wistfully charming as a Victorian calendar picture. She likes my lap as I try to write in longhand. I raise the lapboard, asking, "You're distracting— do you type?" Anything to divert her. "No, but I chew," she purrs. "I especially like your notebook." How can I resist so refined a literary taste? But resist I must or this sentence would end

5

with mew-purr-etaion shrdlu as any printer would tell you. Off you go, miss, into the dawn, until full sunrise.

✼

I find in a small notebook of thirty-five years ago a little composition I wrote while attending a sales conference. Above it I wrote, "Musical notation. Adagio sostenuto." It is in D major, two strains, the second partly a repetition of the first. As I now try it on the violin it is perhaps a little plaintive but not good. Lulled by the chatter about percentages and nets and grosses, Pegasus snoozed on, with only the merest shiver of his wings.

✼

If you do not find civilization where you are, begin it.

✼

Once a big city visitor and I were strolling around the main square of the town I live in. People passed. "Clowns," said my metropolitan friend. "Backwoods yokels. How can you bear the intellectual paucity of this hinterland?" I muttered something.

"But," he said, "just look at that shabby female wretch, that red-faced kook and that stubby little nut." With a serene smile I pointed out that the shabby female was a concert pianist, the kook a Greek scholar turned minister, the nut a distinguished artist. The town was on its toes that day.

✼

It's a friendly town. I decided to smile at everyone I met. Since there are about 20,000 here, there were many strange faces. I got dozens of smiles in return, expressions lighting up in quick succession like fluorescent guideposts along an evening highway.

※

I have many bird neighbors. Once, looking out my office window, at ten of five, I saw a wounded sparrow flopping in the grass at the foot of the portico steps of the next door church.

I thought, "I'll look around for a little box, though I can't leave here until five." I could not find a box. I looked out the window, down at the crumpled bird, then upward. "Well, Sir," I murmured, "if You'll forgive a freethinker, this is it. Your sparrow has fallen." At that instant the young assistant minister came up the church walk, arms full of bundles. He halted, knelt, gathered up the sparrow and went within.

※

Years ago I returned to New England. Every day I'd meet a village selectman, an old-timer. He would never deign to glance my way. But I was reared in New England, so I bided my time. Four years passed. Came a day when the thermometer had risen from 25 to 24 below. I saw the selectman coming along. "Not so cool," says I. "Yup, it's moderatin'," says he. I was in.

※

Idea for science fiction: Green creatures from space learn of our plight, that we'll be wiped out by pollution of our atmosphere. They come to our rescue, but we are so many that only a few million can be transported to their healthy green planet. They ponder—white, red, black, yellow. Finally they decide upon green and take away all of our frogs.

✶

My vote for the gentlest reprimand I ever heard was this. In an office a fellow was working on proofs of a book by a preacher. The latter was present as the editor cut loose with a long string of profanity. "Well," said the preacher with a quiet smile, "I'm glad to see that you've heard the name of our Lord, son."

✶

Personal conflicts as well as those of nation-states arise from the collision of right and right, right and wrong, and wrong and wrong, to balance and adjudicate which we are usually in over our depth and need the deciding vote of an Olympian god, as the old tragedians knew. But Pallas Athena isn't to be seen these days.

✶

Television commercials often teach me what not to buy. If a tycoon comes on and brags that his product is the best because he sells the inferior part of his crop to brokers, he forfeits me as a customer. If competing brands show, name each other and deride the other fellow's brand, guess which brand I buy.

✶

It's on crumbling brown paper, all but indecipherable, a five-year-old pencil scrawl of mine: "On parents day I ackted a monkey in a thing about a owl and monkey." Could be the story of my life.

※※

At eighteen I lived in New York. Then I saw with a painter's eyes because I was studying art. And what would please my adolescent soul more than any treasure in the city of silvery dreams (as it then seemed)? Why, a certain landscape in a deep gilt frame in the New York Public Library. I'd go up the marble stairs ignoring the mural there and reach my private goal and sit before it in peace—a Dutch village in oil, of shadowed trees and mussy, introspective clouds. I forget the painter, but down the spiral staircase of my life I send the little masterpiece my gratitude.

※※

"I read, I wrote, I played," said the American pianist and music critic James Gibbons Huneker, adding that it would make a good epitaph.

※※

Message for a Christmas card: In this holy month, whatever one believes, a memoried scene, simple and touching, arises in one's mind with the utmost tenderness—a Child in a Manger. There are many children in similar humble circumstances even today in India, Pakistan, Bangladesh, the sub-Saharan belt of Africa, Indonesia, Latin America and elsewhere. Fifteen million of them, suffering from malnutrition and starvation, died this year; fifteen million more will die next year. That is one-quarter of the world's annual deaths. The scene in any one of those homes,

9

huts or tents could suggest a lowly Manger, a Christmas crèche —but it would be ghastly.

※

Soon the year will come to its end. Here in the western hemisphere of a small planet in a nameless galaxy we shall hold our tribal festivity. We do it each time the speck called Earth starts a new elliptical journey around the sun. To symbolize this, we pray or drink fermented liquids, and perhaps kiss others who like us are two-legged anthropoids, commonly of the opposite sex. This we do out of universal love and humanity, transcending marital or other restraining compacts, and as such it is vastly relished.

After a day or so of convalescence we remove the Christmas tree, green epitome of something larger than ourselves, and our domestic animals creep to where it was, sniffing to discover what it all meant.

※

I am reading the collected works of two poets. In both lives there is acute suffering. The poems are mirrors reflecting pallid faces, tormented eyes and tears. Poets do not necessarily suffer more than other people, but they sometimes tell about it. We may almost envy those torrents of words, those passionate fingers clutching at the gates of destiny. As I read these poets, one seems never to have gone beyond private experience. We have only a personal portrait. The other has transcended agony, enlarged it to universals and, though finding no ultimate peace, has become a Voice for everyone in need of understanding and courage.

New York newsboys used to yell, "Hey-y-y, the world's on fire!"—waving the edition under your nose. "So's your old man," would have been the retort in the slang of that day. In our nuclear age it would be taken seriously because it might be true.

※

I wonder what Christmas is like Down Under, where it is summer. Does Santa arrive in swimming trunks on a surfboard pulled by a school of dolphins? My encyclopedia tells me everything from aardvark to zygote, but nothing of the children who dream of a green Christmas.

※

One Christmas evening, down in our main square, there was a glowing, revolving scarlet sign in a bank window. It read "$4\,^1/_4$." All around, in other windows, were the usual lights of the season, and a glorious tree over near the Civil War soldier statue. Along came a tot with her mother. Astounded at the most fascinating thing in all the holiday emblazonry, the tot stopped, stared at the "$4\,^1/_4$ per cent"—and sat plunk on her bottom in the snow.

※

Our wood last year was bought from a philosopher. All about his upland place there was a look of woods cultivation, which was just what he was about. Firewood was in neat stacks. He helped us load the trunk of the car.

Later over cider we learned that he had been a professional of advertising and journalism. But soon out came another bent. He

11

reads philosophy. That, he said, is for his inner well-being. The woods work is for outer integration. Our philosophic firewood burned with a special radiance, all winter.

⁂

Men seek a similar equilibrium in the word "ecology." How comforting it would be to believe truly that Nature always maintains a nice ecological balance, and that all would be well if man just behaved himself. But a hungry English sparrow comes to bounce up and down on a twig of the young maple outside this study window, gobbles buds like mad and, since he has no manners, spits out bits he doesn't want.

I think, "Will that ravished twig *be* anything now? I'll watch it nervously, and if the bird comes back I'll rattle the Venetian blind."

Will I really? No. Perhaps he has a secret compact with the maple, and between them they know more than I do.

⁂

Oftentimes I think that Nature wants to tell me something, and is sad that I know the names of things but not what they whisper.

At dawn I went to a window to remark a most curious phenomenon—light. Soundless, it has manifested its presence unbidden by me, and now proceeds to reveal further curiosities that, a few moments earlier, were only a formless murk.

Misted hills are disclosed, one of them like a single Cyclopean eyebrow. "What, still there, little man?" it seems to whisper, and I daresay it had expressed a similar sardonic amusement before the glacier passed over this ancient bowl in the hills.

12

Or it may be silence. As the light increased one morning I saw a large pendant-like branch of our huge silver maple hanging motionless above the windless garden. An arrested moment, eternity.

Perhaps the arts achieve their truest perfection when the total effect is some such stilled eternal symbolism. Thus, the obsidian cat sculpture of Egypt; Hamlet with Yorick's skull; Pavlova at last subsided as the Swan expires.

The year begins to prepare for its final examination. Will it be *cum laude*? I doubt it. The question is whether the world is yet ready to move from Head Start into first grade. *Cum laude* must wait.

I ventured to express a philosophic thought to a distinguished scholar. He inquired, "What is your background?" I said it had been busy but unimpressive. I was wrong. When Virginia Woolf writes, "The butterfly flaunted across the windowpane," she expresses the butterfly more eloquently than might a biologist. A print of a Raphael Madonna hung in a cottage may impart more faith than an entire theology. Even such high symbols as these are not the entire tale of the human spirit. Without the naive thoughts of the humble, uttered through the centuries, we should be poor indeed in soul and mind.

A wasp airlifts across my study. Before I can capture him and let him out he lands behind my long bookcase. I cannot locate him.

Get the insecticide? But I do not want to injure rare editions of Milton, Dante and Molière. So there he dwells, the Wasp in the Bookcase. I concede his victory. After all, he may emerge tomorrow, metamorphosed into a poet.

❧

Of all the arts, musical composition is the most puzzling. In 1773 the seventeen-year-old Mozart composed the divine motet "Exultate," of which the soprano solo is best known, the great "Alleluia." Remarkable? He had composed piano sonatas at seven and a minuet at five. Such potentialities of the human brain are beyond our understanding. It is as if a child had painted the Sistine Chapel frescoes. Not uncommon in music, early genius is rare in other arts. It may be the abstract purity of music, which does not necessarily draw upon experience. Writers and artists trudge the earth; musicians are born with wings.

❧

An old minister once climbed the wintry hill where I lived to ask me to join his church. "But I've not found a formal belief," said I. "I'm still a seeker." "Why, so am I," he replied. "Come along and we'll help each other." I did.

❧

My British foster grandfather would say, "It isn't done." It was his Victorian code of ethics. Often, it persuades me to this day. I do not cheat my neighbor because—"It isn't done." I never gossip—"It isn't done." I will not vote for scoundrels—"It isn't done." Nothing like a bit of old England in one's credo, eh what?

14

January

No man should negatively prejudge his life and labors as having counted for nothing. This—which poet John Keats did not know—is the one conclusion denied to our freedom of thought, since posterity may, with loving sorrow, wish that we had been aware of our worth.

For a man ought to respect the private and best opinion he holds of himself. Most have an inviolable core, that best person we are. I, for example, stubbornly regard myself as a thoughtful man, whose life itself is reward enough, a domain as interesting as the web of a spider. Better than anyone, I know the vibrations of my web; I know its ethereal music in the gentler breezes, its agitation in storm, and what it tells me of the joy and misery of Man.

We are right to live by such affirmings, and by quotations and sayings that, like flotation collars on descended space capsules, buoy and stabilize us. We gather them from parents, grandparents, friends, loves, schools and the world.

My entire generation remembers the optimistic philosophy of a parent, once expressed in these words: "Life is a grand adventure and you're lucky to be having a crack at it."

In this grand adventure I, who am not learned, have studied in vast Athenaeums of mighty Teachers: Boyhood, Love, Sorrow,

Parenthood, Friendship, Beauty, Bereavement, Nature, Work, Hope, and Pain and Ecstasy.

We learn over again the lessons of the past. Michelangelo fretted lest a nephew marry a spendthrift rather than a good dishwasher; Rembrandt was plagued with debt; Hawthorne growled at weather; Balzac had toothaches. It is healthy and clarifying to reflect: "Fate hasn't just singled out *me* for this ordeal."

Life rebuilds. Never shall I cease to believe in its restorative powers. Even homes grow again like perennials. Mark you, even while you mourn the loss of things familiar, replicas one by one appear and silently take their characteristic places, all here again and new in this later emergent time, though only yesterday one was bereft, a person on a corner with a satchel.

To senior citizens: Yours is a threshold facing the morning sun. You have your lifetimes to browse in, like bookstores full of veteran and meaningful tomes. You are sentient organisms under the coruscating blue-whiteness that surrounds Earth, and the whole of Earth's existence is but another book in a vast, galactic library. An ample vista indeed!

Take, for example, an employed person, who goes from home to work and home again, a daily pattern wrought on invisible lines that run between these apogees. Perhaps it is enlarged with small excursions and pleasures. But once retired, one no longer moves on preestablished, invisible lines.

One does things around one's home, explores nearby streets, cultivates a hobby or examines one's skills for self-expression or part-time earnings. It is at last possible to consider the pattern of one's life, who and what one is, and so come to know what Sir Thomas Browne intended when he wrote: "In 70 or 80 years a man may have a deep gust of the world, know what it is, what it can afford, and what 'tis to have been a man."

❧

A man in his late seventies comes slowly with a cane to show me music he has composed. Although frail, his musical zest amazes me—he hums the music, beats time and in a fine state of exhilaration departs, admonishing me to play his composition on my violin as soon as possible.

In the same hour a youth, dressed to the teeth to do student teaching, comes in to ask me things about the Acropolis. I tell him what I know and off he goes loaded with Antiquity, ready to tell of Athens, Dionysos and the Areopagus. I feel as if I had been visited by the gods.

❧

But even when we are cut off from major activity, we may sometimes be of value. In a nursing home in my town an aged woman, almost blind, used to make dusters of multicolored yarns, and down the hall a man paints roses on paper, to be put on the bulletin board to cheer other patients.

Someone wrote that the art of growing old is to do so grace-

17

fully, and Robert Louis Stevenson said: ". . . to settle when the time arrives, into a green and smiling age, is to be a good artist in life and deserve well of yourself and your neighbor."

※

To add to our life-puzzlement, days come up with quite unrelated experiences, like dreams that with bland "logic" include absurdities we accept as natural while asleep.

You dream that you are congratulated by the Supreme Court by telephone, because you have cleaned your stove. The dream goes on to a red stop sign that is, of course, alive, and begins to speak. Then things make sense as the dream becomes a clear remembrance of childhood. But in the next scene you are running through an endless series of rooms in a strange house, after which, most naturally, you find yourself playing a piano concerto at Lincoln Center, to terrific applause—until the hat you are somehow wearing slips down over your nose.

※

Daytime is no less mysterious in its happenchances, all apparently unrelated. We base the choices of our lives upon a few detectable factors only, and we are wrong, since at every moment we are motivated by factors without number. The pigeon whose flight once brushed your cheek—have you thought to include him, although you wist not how he was part of that which urged you here or thither?

※

Events can mystify animals, too. In Boston I saw a cat chase a squirrel down into Charles Street. Instantly struck by a car, the squirrel lay dying. Cars missing it blew it about; soon it was flattened. Death on Charles Street.

This may have been the same squirrel that charmed me as it eluded a cat by going up an outside drain in Louisburg Square. One supposes that Boston squirrels have been dying under wheels of all kinds for generations. Yet this was too good a night for dying, the air being idyllic, the trees enchanted.

Well, next time it will be the cat. It was having a rare time, but stopped astounded as the squirrel did not get up to go on with the game. That was puzzling, and the cat all but arched into a question mark as it turned slowly back up Chestnut Street.

✸

I have been given a tape of Othello's speech to the senators, spoken into a large horn to a wax cylinder, in 1890, by the great Shakespearian actor Edwin Booth. He was ill and weary and found it not easy to speak it "cold" as he said, but he did it for his daughter Edwina, and added the "To be, or not to be" soliloquy from *Hamlet*.

It is greatly moving, this gentle voice, sad and poetic, softly sonorous, rising and falling almost as if in prayer. This is what cannot be taught or acquired, this quality of genius, which simply announces its presence, as in a line of Matisse or the amplitude of an Emily Dickinson poem. Not all the exegesis of scholarship can discover its secret.

✸

All night a pumping crew has worked under bright lights, just as my heart kept pumping as I slept. Who are these watchers of the dark? Braw lads, tapping the street's veins.

19

Roundabout are the softly lightless windows, and we have all dreamed in safety while these steaming benefactors quickened long shadows on the pavements, keeping the pump a-going, systole and diastole, twilight up through galaxies of starlight, until the truck's two lights stared like a sleepless owl at the sun.

✦

I do not know their names. Daily they pass my house, and only a fool would call him unchivalrous because he walks on the inner side of the sidewalk. He has a deeper chivalry. Plainly dressed, carrying his dinner, silent, he goes to work. She walks beside him. Spring and summer, autumn, winter, they go hand in hand.

I think of the Greek myth in which the gods visit a simple home and are given Minerva's olives, wine and wild honey by their lowly hosts, who for their kindness are changed into an oak and a linden, side by side, and each day I think of these my unknown neighbors, with reverence, as Baucis and Philemon.

✦

I am not sure what I believe in, but I am damned sure that Something believes in me or I wouldn't be here.

✦

Out this New Hampshire window I see an elm, builded of many trunks. Sunrise is royal in the upper colonnades of this temple, the sky beyond it a blue of infinity.

Science will name you this tree and the composition of the sky, but not the mystery of them. Before this, Science must yield to you who affirm the mysterious—if not of this world, then in

20

others; if too invisible in all the galaxies, then in other depths of perception, the mystery being everywhere, and supra-physical.

⁂

My daughter, when little, was laboring over a letter to a grand-mother. Desperate, she told me she had no news. "My dear," said I, "letters needn't be news. You simply say anything—your thoughts." Astounded, she tore away at letters to all her relatives and friends, her young mind's Ark opened wide as letters like doves took multitudinous flight.

⁂

Experiment in the arts is the right of any creative person. But one effort seems futile to me. It is the wish to create a synthesis of all the arts in one all-engulfing monstrosity. Opera and the dance try to approach this; modern painting and sculpture, bor-rowing from technics, strain for it; even some modern poetry, by its tortured shape, tries to be the thing it describes. But I have no wish to hear a statue belt out an aria, nor do I want to smell a sonata. We do not need to graft a bluet and an oak to make a better spectacle.

⁂

Once in Concord, Massachusetts, where I was researching for an article on *Little Women*, I interviewed Louisa May Alcott's grandniece, who very much resembled her family of Louisa May's time. I sat in a chair and we chatted. I happened to men-tion Marmee, and my hostess, who sympathized with the trials of Marmee's original, Mrs. Amos Bronson Alcott, said quietly,

"That's Marmee's chair you're sitting in." I felt for my non-existent whiskers to make sure I was not Professor Bhaer, and glanced sharply about, as if I might see Aunt March, Mr. Laurence, Laurie and, giggling in the corner at me, Meg, Jo, Beth and Amy.

✺✺

A Romanian friend, years ago, would smite his forehead when anything happened to him, shouting, "What is this new madness?" It might be love or the end of love, or anything. He wanted life to be one pattern, one simple design. But life is like quicksilver, water, air, music, a billion things and qualities. Still my friend was this much right: We must ask, try to know and understand, and never be creatures of mumbling confusion.

✺✺

If God had said, "Let there be immortality," I'd be the last to deny that He could arrange the mere technical details involved.

February

I was lunching, long ago, with a rather testy trio of gentlemen, all with pretensions of blue blood aristocracy. We fell to discussing what constitutes a gentleman. No aristocrat, I kept a modest silence until the most cruelly arrogant of the group asked me sharply, "Very well, what's *your* definition?"

I was clearly to be exposed for my lack of credentials, as a plebeian whose miserable name did not appear in the platinum-shining records of what passes for our American elite. "The first requisite of a gentleman," said I to my superiors, "is kindness." They stared me up and down with fastidious pity.

To the lonely, any stir of life is welcome. It may be a squirrel, a nurse bringing the meal tray, distant laughter, people chatting across the street—anything that changes silence into sound or stillness into motion, anything that reconnects one with what one was, or may yet be.

It is a moot question, when a person is idle, or not. Late for a banquet, Socrates loitered under a portico "in a fit of abstraction," as Plato tells us. "He just has a habit of stopping anywhere and losing himself without any reason." No reason? Part of our own is owed to the genius of that reasoning mind. A seeming idler was Jean Henri Fabre, French entomologist, idly watching caterpillars tailgating around the rim of his pool. He was gathering data for his lifelong study of instinct. The artist Jean François Millet would look at an old wheel for hours. He was thought mad, but *The Angelus* hangs in the Louvre.

Often, as I sit in my study, I look just over there at my long bookcase. In front of it stood a young man on December 26, 1964, telling me with quiet earnestness of his life plans. I wrote in this journal the next day, "He is a lad whose career I've watched for some years with respect, though that is not quite it—rather, a feeling that he would become something fine." His name? Jonathan M. Daniels.

Once I bought a guppy for companionship. Naming it Octavia —though why I called her after Nero's wife I don't know—I placed her bowl on my coffee table, made a drink and sat down, with a gratefully whimsical speech in mind. But Octavia was lying belly up. Perhaps she'd been lonely, too, and I was not quite the answer. As befitted the demise of a Roman empress, I took her by the tail to the garden, stuck my forefinger into the good Earth and put her to rest.

So you want to be a poet, an inventor—or anything? Then lift your face and think, "I am a poet"—or whatever. Name you to yourself. Thenceforth you inhabit a new world, if you mean it. The naming, the commitment, comes first.

※

In a novel by the celebrated French author, the late Colette, the reader's first glimpse of the heroine is when, as she awakes in the morning, her right arm arises like a sinuous cobra in the sunlight. She is remembering her lover. Nothing more is described. When the explicit writing of today has been forgotten, the finesse of Colette will be effective still, the uplifting white arm a work of art like the *Bird in Space* sculpture of Brancusi.

※

When I was young I lay in a Catholic hospital, recovering from an appendectomy. A growling old Irish priest would first hear the confessions of five others in my ward, then come with mock ferocity to me, a Protestant, and say, "Well, son, and what can I do for you today?" Boldly, skeptical adolescent that I was, I asked him to prove to me the existence of God. Without a word he held up one hand, jiggled the little finger up and down, patted my nose and left with a wink.

※

Returned from Athens, a student neighbor brings me a bit of Pentelic marble from the Acropolis. He does it to please me, though I could wish he had not done so, since ancient Greece is already in my heart and needs no tangible proof. Even had he found a fleck of gold there, long fallen from the statue of Athena,

I should prefer it left, a talisman of wisdom, however small, brave and bright in the rubble.

❦

Some years past I was amongst the basses in a cantata. My untrained second-bass voice could not get as high as middle C. I asked our conductor about it and was told to drop out rather than transpose an octave down, and he said, "We'll need you in the lower range," thereby preserving for me a sense of particular usefulness. To leave another secure in a special area may be as great a principle of ethics as the Golden Rule.

❦

I found myself at a table of ancestor worshipers. "Old family" was the expression that oftenest came up. As the one-upmanship grew competitive, a minister at my right inquired mildly of the group, "But doesn't *everyone* come from an old family?"

❦

A guest tells me earnestly that she is studying speed-reading. "It may have its merits," said I, "but I study to read more and more slowly, savoring every word. Once I read Dryden's translation of Virgil's *Aeneid*, every line twice before going on. It took three months." To read only for speed is like going through the Louvre on a motorcycle.

❦

Slowness has other merits. My father, an artist, would take me to an art gallery. "Now," he'd say, "the trick of looking at a painting is to pick a spot in the middle and look at it hard and count sixty—slowly. Then you look around at the rest of it. You can walk right into it." Can't do that on a motorcycle.

❧

A fanciful start for a period novel is teasing me: "Armeline Vorth, up in her dressing gown at four, pinned a yellow carnation to the left lapel, lighted her spirit lamp and went to her standing desk at the tall Gothic window." Jane Austen or Virginia Woolf could have taken off from there. But I'm afraid that I must forget Armeline and leave her standing, imperiously alone, non-existent forever. She's yours, anyone.

❧

Daily we live our lives as facts only, go here, go there, buy, sell, eat, love, ail, clean house, go to work, taking part in all the rituals of our kind. Rarely do we consider the inner qualities of our days, finding universals in the passing moment. In his life of Emerson, Van Wyck Brooks wrote that when one can see the poetry in the affairs of the day, "the dry twig blossoms in the hand."

❧

Henry David Thoreau, symbol of ideal solitude, was rarely alone. Off to the village and supper he went frequently, from Walden Pond, or to his bean field to chat with passing farmers on the Boston turnpike. Ice cutters, fishermen, poets, philosophers, mice and birds frisked in his populous woodland. Henry had only to

27

shout—the answer would be that of a living man, pounding a railroad tie or muttering the lines of an epic poem.

※

Mine host at a dinner party tells me that he'd never forgotten how once in his presence I wrote a poem while seated under a tree. He said this with a kind of reverence. I may thus have inspired a man's life, yet I do not recall the time, the poem or the tree. In the same way I have been inspired by people who must have gone their mundane ways, unaware that they had left with me a mental marker saying "Thither."

※

Khufu, Khufra, Menkaura—who were they? Gigantic tombs mark where they were placed for eternity, their fame supposedly deathless. Yet most of us know only the tombs, the Pyramids at Gizeh, Egypt. The monarchs' names mean little if anything to us. Then there was a man whose body was flung in a snowstorm into a paupers' vault containing twenty coffins, in the churchyard of St. Mark's, Vienna. His was never identified. But the world still loves Mozart's music and plays it daily everywhere.

※

As a child I believed that America was settled by the Pilgrims at Plymouth Rock. For me, the rest of the continent was dense forest, perilous and unknown. What I was not told was that about forty others had explored the country from Newfoundland to California, and from Bering Strait to Tierra del Fuego.

28

Say, like Hernando de Soto, who in 1539 was—where? Why, up the Mississippi, near Memphis.

I begin to grasp, a little, the descriptions of the DNA molecules, the helical wonders that determine the structure and functioning of our bodies. I dare not guess, however, at the fearful molecular or other foreknowledge that tells a robin a worm is just below the surface, makes a beaver build a dam and whispers faith into the future brain of a human being.

When whole groups are labeled left, right, center, establishment, anti-establishment, hippie, hard hat, etc., I am skeptical. Among all of these, I have found only people. In a wartime shipyard I once, as a shipfitter, withdrew a heavy jack holding in place a header inside the shell, at main deck level, when I lost balance and began to fall to the double bottom. A giant Creole welder, squatting huge beside me, scooped me out of the air with a long, slothlike arm, and we went up on deck to smoke, have coffee and talk in French. He'd heard that I wrote, said his life would make a book and asked me how to begin it. I quoted Arnold Bennett: " 'My dear man, you simply begin.' " I hope he did.

Some who have influenced the world with their words never wrote anything. Such was Epictetus, Greek philosopher of about 60 A.D. His pupil Flavius Arrianus transmitted much of his teaching. Such also was Socrates, who comes to us only through

29

Xenophon and Plato. Then there was a Man of Nazareth, whose words have come to us through certain fishermen, a tax collector and a physician.

We greet the dying of winter as if it were never to be resurrected. Spring, summer and fall are longed for as if the first did not bring dangerous illnesses after the exhaustion of the cold months, the second torpid heat, the last its celebrated melancholy. The truth is that every season has its price, as does every human condition. We are as migratory as wild geese, though we project our journeys in qualities instead of time and space, and forever tease our minds to conjure a better Eden just over there, or left behind, but never quite here. When we do find it here we are unprepared for surprise and joy, and are almost grateful for adversity, for ease of conscience.

SPRING

March

Five crows, frock-coated in dignity, have arrived and sit upright and still on a bough. One thinks, "Oh, beloved symbols of New England" or "Drat those birds," depending upon whether one is planning a poem or a cornfield. A gentle old-timer tells me how the sight of a crow heartened him when he was employed in Boston. New England abounds in cherished symbols: the crow, brook, tree, rock, barn, mill, marsh, pond, robin, meaningful since childhood, and pervading the arts and letters of this region. After a quarter century returned from megalopolis I still cannot get enough of them.

What if one gave up caring! Suppose total indifference—would that be peace? To shrug at good and evil, to feel numb about life, love, death, the woes of others, and to turn from beauty and truth as hopeless dreams too long sovereign in our hearts? I can think of nothing more frightening than to be concerned with only Me, lacking these wider thoughts. May I always be burdened with tribulation, always inspired with hope, not excluding the final enigma of Thee.

In the one-room schoolhouse at Westminster, Connecticut, decades ago, I was the only eighth grader. Our teacher was Ruth

Shorter, a soft-spoken girl with dark Renaissance eyes and parted black hair drawn back to a knot. I was to recite the opening lines of William Cullen Bryant's "Thanatopsis":

> "To him who in the love of Nature holds
> Communion with her visible forms, she speaks
> A various language. . . ."

I recited but said I did not understand it. Then my teacher, who died fifteen years later in a fire, told me about the poem with such perceptive sensitivity that for me the day was transfigured. She never knew how for one pupil she had raised a curtain on the whole, wide, lovely and tragic realm of life and thought.

The late W. H. Auden said that poetry and the other arts are only "fun" and do not alter the course of history. I disagree. I believe in the long-range efficacy of the arts, as a gentling influence in the stream of mankind, without which we would be far worse savages than we are.

A certain Puckish, scholarly old law professor used to ramble on peaks of thought, about Jurisprudence, not to say the greater Alps of Justice and the nature of the Good.

His literal-minded students ground their teeth—they had come to learn about practical law, the face-to-face nitty-gritty of the courtroom, not the love of human justice.

If you are a writer and can write but one word a day, in a year you will have 365, in twenty years about 7,300. Meagre? That is 2,300 more than the Chinese philosopher Lao-Tse wrote in his lifetime.

An automobile mail-order house has sent me its catalogue, I who have very little notion of what makes my car go, and suspect the presence under the hood, of a little gray gnome who runs and runs. I see that I may buy horns that will bray like a donkey, whinny like a mustang, whistle like a wolf or play "Oh, Susanna." Now if they only had one that would snort like a Senior Citizen . . .

The Onion is a creature of great and mystic beauty, a glorious bulb that could only have been created in one of Heaven's most exalted moods. The exquisiteness of the Onion brings tears smarting with gratitude, while the nose already senses the final feast, the taste buds frolic, and the smooth little planet hefts delightfully on the palm. But I have had Onions in lamb stew, Onion soup for lunch, Onions in pot roast, Onions in party hors d'oeuvres, and this is Onion omnipresent and the sovereign devil of my guts. I can have too much of an oratorio, and alas, too much of the celestial bulb, the Onion.

Like solemn ghouls, biographers for decades have made varying guesses, all inferred and none proven, as to the man who was presumably loved by Emily Dickinson, the Amherst, Massachusetts, poet who died in 1886. Never in literary history have so many pecked and dug at the sacred privacy of so great and sensitive a person, as if, having exposed her heart, the world might know the secret of her genius. One could reverently desire that, on the iron grillwork fence within the small enclosure of which she sleeps, there were a small plaque, with her own words:

"On her divine majority
Obtrude no more."

Humming, undistraught, a lad tangles his kite string on the maple outside my study window. He works at it as if with quiet curiosity, then breaks the string, once more attaches the red kite to a ball of string and is off, the kite just missing elms. This is the very grist of poetry, but I am not a poet. Were I, the lost string would be that which the lad has come to see he must leave behind. Presently he may learn what it is to see the kite aloft in tatters. I shall hope that he will still be humming, undistraught, and go on to fly the kite of life with courage.

Apple trees are mad. Their branches grow wildly, caricaturing the forms of other trees. One branch goes aloft to play at being a maple and ends in a preposterous wiggle. Another is a clown parodying a dancer. Others pretend to be brambles. Some are bunchy, some pompous, and some are showers or curved spears aimed at the earth. And all these on one small tree! Yet out of this frenzy, this daft, grimacing jester of a tree, will come blossoms of demure perfection and shining symmetries of fruit.

A sister of mine says that it is the obligation of those who can express themselves to do so, since often they may put into words what others feel and cannot describe. It is a beautiful but eerie responsibility; it is also one to be honored with humility—if a man thinks that he and only he can speak for all mankind, he becomes a messianic madman.

* * *

Live now so that every object is burnished with meaning and beauty. Cherish existence!—all the arts and sciences and thoughts of Man have not exhausted its inner richness.

* * *

We live within history, in what will become Antiquity. It is difficult to believe it, since we live at a time when all can be obliterated forever by nuclear warfare. But if *homo sapiens* controls this, we should, if we could know in future ages, much regret that we had disbelieved in our part in history, and had refrained in despair from recording the fruits of our lives and asking the eternal questions.

* * *

When my father was a boy in Ohio his father found him sketching and fetched a chromolithograph of the Venus di Milo, saying, "Draw that." Dad did and his father took him to a carriage painter. Dad became his paint boy. While not busy on carriage decoration or a large canvas, the painter began to instruct the small blond lad, seating him before an easel with a piece of charcoal. Dad, whose name was Reuben, was too shy to try, until the painter stood behind him, saying gently, "Make your hands go, Ruby." He did and became an artist. I always liked the story's end. The painter was A. M. Willard, and the large canvas he was working on was one of his versions of *The Spirit of '76*.

✦

The patient, sympathetic nurturing of talent is the mark of all fine teachers. As a former editor I affirm that this is true of that calling, too. Long ago I succeeded the late Charles Agnew Mac-Lean as editor of *The Popular*, a once-celebrated fiction magazine. MacLean was a soft-spoken erudite Scot, beloved by his writers. When he died, many wrote gratefully about him.

One, Percival Wilde, said: "He was one of the gentlest gentlemen I ever knew. It was given to Charles Agnew MacLean to love humankind in such an unselfish manner that the success of another was to be rejoiced in as if it were his own success; and I never knew a man who thought and spoke more sympathetically and tolerantly of those whom destiny willed to turn out failures." My own debt to MacLean is beyond words.

✦

At the clinic the patients went in one by one for treatment of fractures, broken limbs, and such, each with his or her white cast on arm or leg. Finally only a few waiting relatives, like myself, were left. A nurse appeared and called, "Benjamin ———" The last name was as impressive as the first. I glanced about, expecting a tall, distinguished gentleman. But no one answered. The nurse tried again, "Benjamin ———?" This time with a questioning expression. Then there arose from the floor, where she had been amusing Benjamin, a young mother who, after lifting him to one shoulder, carried him in. He was a charming child of about two, wearing a full leg cast, and as they passed where I sat he smiled down at me like the infant Mercury.

As children in school we learn more than the tasks before us. Surreptitiously gawking out windows, I went on voyages unknown to my teachers—to the tops of trees, the deeps of woods, down the wriggling freshets of spring and past the utmost horizon. The schoolhouse windows were books, too, though I got no marks for what they taught me, unless it were a zero for my idling. Idling! I was as busy as Magellan.

April

Music, I think, began for me when I was five. A great-grand-uncle came to visit. I was expecting a Personage, akin to royalty. He arrived, a small, ill-shaven, wizened man in a dusty suit and derby. He had presents. Mine was a harmonica. It may have been two inches long; it seemed a foot. It may have been a toy store trinket; with its gleaming tin it looked like a cathedral organ, and it bore the word Hohner, or it may have been Handel, incised in old English, with scrolls at the ends. My introduction to music, then, was less aural than visual. The beautiful word in the shiny tin filled me with awe. I like to fancy that, from over the barn and past the flaglilies below the house, scarcely audible but silvery true in pitch, I heard the Hallelujah Chorus of the *Messiah*.

I am fond of whimsical sayings that probably mean nothing, like "Heigh-ho, saith the woodcock," and "To the rocks with carking Care," and this:

> "To wander, fancy free, the enchanted way
> Where elves do dwell with Robin Goodfellow."

Also I like "In this place, too, men have found the materials of life." I've never identified the sources of these, although I think the last may be John Bunyan.

40

You won't find it in the dictionary, but in my family we call it a pillywig. It is anything you keep around—preferably a small object—for sentimental or inspirational reasons. In my study as I look about I see two Chinese figurines; a bit of stonewall from my home town; a small piece of quartz that makes me think of Emerson's grave, marked with the large pink quartz; a saucer full of beach shells and stones; my father's last palette; and a plaster reproduction of one of the gold Vaphio cups of 1500 B.C., found near Sparta.

⁂

I turn on a newscast. The world roars into my ears. How vast a distance it is from the slow past, when news took months to cross an ocean. Men lived then with an illusory sense of a world status quo that often no longer existed. Winter could pass and spring come before one learned that an empire had fallen, a pestilence had destroyed a civilization or a new philosophy had created a totally different era. Still, there was time to have unhurried thoughts about crops and destiny, and take one's own pace at an embroidery or a castle in the air.

⁂

After we are gone, others will have our passionate sense of being "I" and will adore dawn, kneel at brooks, pet a child, write a poem and stroll about dazed with love. Others will play music, pray, sip a drink, open a marvelous book and dream of the golden future. Sadly, too, in that "tomorrow and tomorrow," there will be tragedy, pain, fear, but it would be folly not to consider also the blossoming meadow and the deep voice of a concerto grosso, both still vividly part of life. We shall have future counterparts recognizable and lovable, could we know them.

As I remember all the rooms, flats, apartments and houses of my life, each is an entity, a crucible in which that life has been formed. In each the slowly evolving destinies of a number of people were built, word by word, meal by meal, act by act, hope becoming despair, despair again replaced by hope. There is more than we discern in the moment, were we able to project its role in the full context of our lives.

Occasionally I fear that I read too many fine morals or universal principles into things. If I pick up a beer bottle someone has tossed on my lawn, the matter is not necessarily of Homeric proportions. One may, as Emerson did, find all history in a nut-shell, but we cannot so preoccupy our vision with every nut that falls from a tree. Most nuts are content to be nuts, not blueprints of epochs.

Your least thought, expressed to someone, may pass into the life-stream, be repeated as a saying, an adage, and become a part of the ocean of the human mind, now and then bobbing to the surface, a timely hope or guide for a lost seafarer of existence.

Beware the gentle essayist. He sidles up to you and deftly whispers a life philosophy into your ears. Heed him not, the rascal is out to change the universe. I scarcely know what I am because of the dulcet and irresistible importunings of such cunning fellows as Montaigne, Pascal, Lamb, Emerson, Thoreau, Huneker, Stevenson, to mention only a few of these rogues in the crowd.

They espied me, a lean and soulful lad, drew me apart and jingled each his bag of bright trinkets, from which I selected those I loved and in secret hung them in my mind, where to this day they swing like miniature lights of all colors, some as small as candles, others larger than the largest stars.

Since I have no money to spend on a collection of books or works of art, I collect dawns. To do so requires no unique expertise—I am merely an early riser.

The little cars mailmen ride in nowadays make me think of the postman in my boyhood in Canterbury, Connecticut. He'd come uphill in his white, high, skinny wagon, which had a door and step on one side. It was drawn by a bay horse with a fixed grin as if it loved its work. We were expecting my aunt on a Wednesday. Uphill came the horse, wagon and postman. He was waving a card and calling, "She can't come Wednesday, she's comin' Friday!" Kinda neighborly.

The late David Morton of Deerfield, Massachusetts, a poet of rare beauty and depth, said in a poem that one should confront "collapse and chaos" with "the grave, compulsive word," before which chaos must "turn and flee." We act on our times on many levels, and this is one of them. It is a long, slow effect, but it is the best, as it is uttered in our faiths, our social integrity, our private honor. All these begin in the individual. No evils can forever withstand an upwelling of moral excellence in the general will.

❧❧

One healthy result of the energy crisis may be that we shall come to know better our immediate environment. How long has it been since we espied the first arbutus,

"Firstborn of the wayward Spring,"

—as my mother called it in a poem? In another context Thoreau remarks, "If you are chosen town clerk, forsooth, you cannot go to Tierra del Fuego this summer." But the universe is at our doorsteps nonetheless.

❧❧

One of my violin teachers was Martin Conway, who came to America after a strange double career in the French Foreign Legion and as a first violinist with the Scottish Symphony Orchestra. He would have me play, hold his ears, rush out, then come back and play the piece for me. One solo I studied was Robert Schumann's "Traumerei," which I loved. When Maestro Conway returned to Glasgow, he said he would not announce his arrival to his family, who would be having a New Year's Eve gathering of the clan at his ancestral home. He would burst in at midnight, hush them as they began to greet him and say, "Now first before I join you I want to play 'Traumerei' for a laddie in America." I was to stay up until the equivalent hour and think of what he'd be doing. Never do I play it without remembering, and almost I can believe that I heard it that wintry night, across the Atlantic.

44

If we ail, our doctor with his folder full of our case is Mission Control, but we, with high morale, must fly the ship.

⁂

Whatever else this April brings, it comes with a sense of a Promised Land attained after the dark winter of threatened fuel shortage. My fireplace has never seemed so vital a part of life, even though, at least as this is written, it was not, after all, needed for emergency heat and cooking. But never again can it deceive me that it is purely decorative, despite its charming white Corinthian-columned mantel. We are henceforth bound together, fireplace and I, and before next winter I may find a way to suspend a kettle and a cooking pot therein, like any foresighted pioneer, lacking only a wild turkey out yonder and a blunderbuss.

⁂

A distinguished scholar tells me that he and a colleague once decided that in retirement they would no longer read books about books, but only go back to original works. Should I do it, too, I wonder if I should not miss the spring morning ecstasy of youthful discovery, when this or that great mind became a glory for the first time in my eager head. Now as I re-open some such original, I fear that I have trudged to it, bearing the load of all my life and endeavor, denying me that sudden and marvelous vista of new demesnes.

⁂

Once it lived in deep Atlantic waters, on the bottom, trapping plankton. Hurtled to a beach it dried, turning white but still

45

keeping its shell pattern, like a five petaled-blossom. Some call it a Sea Biscuit, others a Sand Dollar, because it is about the size of a silver dollar. I have no idea how long it withstood ocean and tempest, this little skeleton, but Man's ways were too much for it. Brought to my home, it became a window decoration, and fell and broke. I'll try to repair it. That would seem the least one might do, a small propitiating office for one of Neptune's loveliest flower children.

May

At my kitchen doorstep fiddlehead ferns arise in groups, all facing each other as if agog about what other plants are up to. My suspicions thus aroused, I look for trouble. Sure enough, a dandelion has blossomed nearby. Tulips threaten to do the same. Iris send up shafts of naked green. Lilacs scheme to take over, and a robin hops from behind a daffodil, no doubt a Redcoat we were warned about by Paul Revere. Clearly the ferns have set themselves to gossiping madly about the meaning of all this cultural revolution.

From my boyhood home I filch a small three-inch stone, a fragment of an old wall beside a meadow. It is spotted with gray-green lichen. How old this rock is I do not know—but not more than I am since in my earthly components I am just as venerable. Now perhaps it and I are as interesting as any from the moon, even though scientists the world over are not eager, at least right now, to dissect us.

I have a man plow my small vegetable plot. He tells me, and I harken with pleasure, of the days when he drove a two-horse team. I go and buy a bag of fertilizer and chat with another man who was once a farmer.

Returned home, I rake in the fertilizer and sit down puffing from such unsedentary exertion. But I am as peaceful as if I had been given a $100 bill. Why a man may feel so, I could tell you, but it would take as long as to read the *Georgics* of Virgil or 100 years of the *Old Farmer's Almanac*.

An oblong of marble sat for generations at the foot of my front walk. The city asked permission to take it away to make things easier for the snow plow. I had them push it back into the garden, where it rests near a gnarled hydrangea, resembling a marker for the grave of a beloved family horse. Grasses have accepted it and there it sits, I hope for eternity. Eternally, too, in my imagination, the ghosts of long ago children stand tiptoe on it, greeting Mamas arriving in the buggy; wraiths of newlyweds ascend thereon, pelted with invisible rice from my wooden Doric porch, and aged forms, like mists, stoop to praise it for easing their goings and comings.

Materials from earth became a man—although I do not limit him to this—and with other products of earth he wrote music with a quill pen and paper. Three hundred years later still other men, playing upon other things from the soil, recorded the music, metals from the ground became a tower on a hill, and now through time and air I hear a beautiful concerto, via still more earth materials, an FM stereo. It is as if an unplowed field had stirred to life in a magical ancient dawn.

In the clinic lab waiting room one morning I counted six gray-haired men, myself one of the graying, and a gray-haired lady, awaiting their turn for blood tests, cardiograms or X-rays as the case might be. This is that brother-and-sisterhood of pathology of which I was so little aware in my younger years, yet even then there was the procession coming one by one to such realities of life. Not that all, as I waited, were gray. I saw a girl—seventeen? twenty?—sitting there, her eyes confused with apprehension or deeper fear, and no one was with her to allay her troubled mind.

✿

The full moon casts on a next door house the shadow of our silver maple. It lies on the white clapboards and tile roof at a slant, like a living thing, huge as a Loch Ness monster, yet a monster asleep and at rest, alone in the night. I peer with awe from a window, scarce able to believe that so strange a shadowgraph has taken possession of my modest garden, and I resume my chair and predawn coffee with an eerie but comforting sense of a Presence, just out there, silent.

✿

To the groaning sound of saws, a great elm is being felled from the top down. It is doubtless the best way, but I prefer the way a noble tree was once allowed to fall, still majestic with dignity.

✿

Lewis Mumford said that the world needs a great new inspiration. But Walter Lippmann held that we must not hope for a new revelation, that we already have the principles of a good society stored in our memories, in the religions and ethical thought of all our human centuries.

When I was seventeen, besides my throes, I found it a time of shimmering beauty, too. Life was half dream, a time of feeling unique, special. Was there anyone who could understand? Had no one felt as I did about day, night, poetry, love? Then I grew, and light overspread the dream, like morning sun dimming the high coasting moon, and at long last, with relief and joy, I knew that I was not alone, but legion.

An office colleague of mine, years ago, scorned classical music as "longhair." As he worked he would whistle over and over, a musical theme. I could not bear to tell him—it was the opening of the Tchaikowsky First Piano Concerto.

It delights me to read, in Cicero, "I have in my hand my seventh book of Antiquities." He was collecting, he said, materials for a history of Rome, which he never wrote. In his lifetime (106–43 B.C.) people looked back just as we do, to a deeply ancient past. Cicero looked back to Rome's beginning in about 700 B.C. That was as if we should think of the time of Magna Carta (1215 A.D.). If Cicero thought back over years comparable with ours to his, he would have been thinking of the Minoan Age in Crete.

Honeyboy the Cat proceeds to the kitchen and sneers at the fine supermarket fare I've dished out for him. He comes to my study to inform me with silent contempt that such a Cat as himself, with gray coat, white cravat and yellow eyes, merits nothing but caviar and pressed duck. Any fool knows that, he tells me, with patricianly restive movements of his forefeet. Here I pull rank: I stamp one foot like a horse, whereat he concedes that he is, after all, just an alley cat from the Humane Society, and slinks to the foul breakfast muttering.

"Walking the boundary" is an old New England custom. Perhaps it is done elsewhere. But we ought to walk our abstract boundaries, too, from time to time, to study whence we have come and whither we tend. How do we fare in our beliefs, relationships, aims? Does underbrush obscure our life-markers, those invisible pegs or pipes or upended stones by which we know our duties, limitations and possibilities? For a life is like a tract of property.

In a letter on May 10, 1838, to Thomas Carlyle, Ralph Waldo Emerson wrote: "I occupy, or IMPROVE, as we Yankees say, two acres only of God's earth. . . ." Do we improve this tract of our nature, or is it a tangle of brambles and dead wood? Then it is time to walk the boundary yet again.

I have brought back from a Connecticut visit a clump of yellow, five-sepaled marsh marigold, in green moss and sopping brookside soil. Potted, it is doing well. And what indeed have I toted home? Nothing less than the "Mary-bud" of Shakespeare, and here it is in *Cymbeline*, Act II, Scene 3 . . . "and winking Mary-buds begin to ope their golden eyes."

※

James Gibbons Huneker (1860–1921), American critic, wrote in a dazzling style as he alerted this country to the New Spirit, as it was called, in European arts, music and letters. Havelock Ellis (1859–1939), English psychologist, wrote in a sunlit, luminous prose, of which his *Impressions and Comments* is a masterly example. To Ellis, Huneker wrote: " 'Impressions and Comments' I have by me every night; it contains the quintessence of Ellis, of the philosophy and poetry and a general attitude that is for me so consoling in the midst of vulgarity, triviality and terror." Huneker's *Intimate Letters* and Ellis' *Impressions and Comments* stand side by side in my bookcase. I hope they know.

※

Last October I journalized: "The overcast sky now begins to have its calligraphy of linear trees and leaves lie on earth as if painted there. In a Fall mood I turn over translations (by others) of Martial, Propertius and other Latin poets, praising loves and sorrowing for the dead." Now winter's linear aspect gives way to the paint of Spring, as if the leaves had flown to their perches in coats of green. And the Latin poets? They, and all other such, remain at our call, ready to reclothe the linear starkness of civilization.

※

The late Arturo Toscanini said that in music it is your right to like what you like and dislike in turn, and you needn't know why or apologize.

"I insist that you keep your presence of mind while passing through Newark," a parent wrote me long ago when I was in an emotional quandary. "Newark" was only a word symbol for a transitory phase of life. There is always more to come. An anguished Now, as time goes by, becomes a muted Then, what loomed so has lost its power, and we are glad indeed if presence of mind brought us to a peak of mental perspective from which we might espy the future landscape of our journey.

＊＊＊

She took my adult education creative writing course, years ago. Desperately shy, tearfully apologetic, she said that she had no right to be there among "all these real writers." Finally she tried a short story about a sad little boy and doggedly revised it nine times. Last December she died, a gentle soul, an uncertain, diffident spirit longing to express itself—and succeeding. It was the best story of the class.

＊＊＊

At the Longfellow—or Craigie House as it is also called—in Cambridge, Massachusetts, I marveled at the extensive library, and felt sad in the living room where his second wife, the gracious Frances Appleton Longfellow, was fatally burned while applying sealing wax to a letter. Then I entered his study, which is intact down to the last ink sander and paperweight. As I looked about, in rushed a bevy of schoolgirls, happy, chattering, irreverent. He would have wanted that, for were they not just so many Alices, Allegras and Ediths, grave, laughing or golden-haired, as his own had been, and of whom he wrote in "The Children's Hour?"

Good conversation is best when characterized by warm mutual concern or appreciation. One puts forth his own best but readily yields the floor. It is important to respond, compliment, encourage, provide feedback. Perhaps this is only good manners, but it is also a recognition that we need the minds of others. As in a mosaic, many parts are needed to complete the design of the whole.

❧

"Oil front door for squeak." So it says on the pad beside my typewriter. So I've done it. Egad, I do know a mechanical trick or two. I've been known to repair a lamp, am skilled at restringing a violin and once I fixed a typewriter with a rubber band and a paper clip. It lived on for years. Shakespeare has Prospero in *The Tempest* say, "We are such stuff as dreams are made on," but there are times when we are happier without a squeak, a darkened lamp, a fiddle out of tune or a typewriter that is stuck. Dreams can wait a minute or two.

❧

We suppose that our lives are structured by schools, jobs, housekeeping and all the tangible things acquired as we go along. There is much else besides, of course. But lurking in all these are the good hours, in which we have a sense of something more than facts. Here and there are moments with a nimbus-like halo, a central beauty and meaning, all but indescribable, strange, memoried, delicate as the scent of a mayflower and as brief. Such moments are the companion-spirits of our years, the essences that have made life worth its care and toil. All gone? In the past? No, if you will greet them, they will meet you today.

At a lecture's end there was unveiled a replica of the bust of Egypt's fourteenth-century B.C. Queen Nefretete (it is spelled several ways). Here was a beauty we can understand, nothing less than the latest fashion model, aloof and cool, an international jet-set type, long of neck and wearing the latest Parisian head-gear. She is a symbol of the eternal ideal, glimpsed in part from palaces to cornfields. But the search need not be arduous—anyone we truly love is the young Queen Nefretete even though she is to become a centenarian tomorrow.

✿✿✿

With no surprise, I find many changes in my opinions in my journals of the past forty years. Nonetheless, a journal is not an exercise in idle inconsistencies, it is an organic thing, a mind speaking to itself and, hopefully, ever growing.

✿✿✿

What would ancient Greeks at the Olympiads have thought of our streaking this spring? A healthy trend long overdue in a Puritan society? Or unhealthy, as contrasted to the bronzed and naked athletes at Olympus? And I seem to recall a picture of swift Atalanta, stooping to pick up one of the apples of the Hesperides, in her famous race. Even the gals got into the act. None of them could have associated the beauty of the body with stealth and defiance of convention.

✿✿✿

The truly great are human and unaffected. I saw Fritz Kreisler enter at Carnegie Hall, holding his violin by the scroll at knee

55

length as if he were toting, by its leaves, a garden carrot. At a benefit concert in the old Metropolitan Opera House I heard the contralto Ernestine Schumann-Heink, aged, tall, majestic, a monolith of greatness. As she finished she tousled the hair of the concertmaster and others, perhaps remembering her sons, killed in World War I. Long before that, had you been in Concord, Massachusetts, you could have seen a spare, shawled man waiting patiently in line to mail a letter—neighbor Ralph Waldo Emerson.

SUMMER

June

As I sit in my garden a hornet witchhunts the air, a bee growls that I trespass, ants patrol my feet, a spider descends from a branch to inspect my credentials, a mosquito bayonets me and black flies try to make a Pearl Harbor of my face. Shall I call them friends, Hiawatha's chickens? Rather, I'd like to impale them on pins, under glass. Even in my most Albert Schweitzerian mood of love for all things, I am forced to concede that, as someone said, this is not the Age of Man but of the Insect.

I look, and look again, at morning sunlight on a tall shrub. The shrub appears to have doubled its size because the light has painted it a golden kind of green and added a shadow of startling intensity on the green wall of the house behind it. Were I scientific there'd be no problem as to which is which, but as an imaginative sort I face the old Platonic dilemma of the real and the shadow of the real, which are not so readily differentiated.

Keepers of journals rarely do so in idyllic solitude, like that in the quasi-autobiographical—and delightful—*The Private Papers of Henry Ryecroft*, by George Gissing. I've added to my own on buses, trains, ferries, even street corners, in odd moments of a life of editorial deadlines. I have never found, or wanted, a secluded door of utter apartness and serenity, shut to the world. Rather, a door ajar, that admits far sounds of the seven continents like the sea one hears in a shell, the distant surge of peoples, my kin from here to the Antipodes.

⚜

I like to enlarge my provincial American mind. When Massachusetts and Virginia were being "discovered" by the English, the supposed savages of the New World were not the whole story. In 1585 over 300 poets had competed in a vice-regal contest in Mexico.

⚜

In childhood we do not know what "co-extensive" means, but it is the special marvel of that time. It meant the feel of sand underfoot, the cool branch of a maple, the taste of berries along a hot wayside, sky up through corn, the witchery that made a bike the finest horse in Christendom. We were like plants that had grown hands and feet, or animals but just arisen from plant existence at a creek's edge. It was as if we ourselves were Nature, as indeed we were, and might even be again if we could drop our innocence and return to that sublime sophistication.

⚜

Pride in ancestry might quail at an actual forebear. Perchance, arriving through time, he might leap from his dragon-headed ship, a brute with a bloody spear, and with a demonic yell

60

shatter the door, cart off the dainty silver and heirlooms and go howling away with the lady of the house shrieking in his arms. One doubts if a survivor would restore the coat of arms to its place above the mantelpiece.

⚜

A very old person used to tell of the halcyon days of childhood. People were polite, children obedient, crime unknown and flowers were better and more plentiful.

The fairytale was probably a comfort, but she was recollecting the decade of the 1880s to 1890 when 900,000 perished in a Chinese flood, the Opéra Comique burned in Paris with 200 lost, the Haymarket riots erupted in Chicago, the Battle of Wounded Knee was fought and first electrocution was carried out at Auburn, New York. The idyll of childhood depended upon our ignorance of adult realities around us.

⚜

If the galaxies are a pointless scampering of blind forces, and we a queer accident of reasoning life, then what an accident! We are then a strange intelligence created by blind force which can observe it. Could anything be more eerie? It is as if a phial were filled with hydrogen atoms, amongst which mysteriously appeared an Eye!

⚜

It is creative suicide to hop a bandwagon. There are monetary rewards, and then—oblivion. How much better is the independence of the late Mark Van Doren's poetry, never yielding to

61

the fashion of obscurantism. And how sad is the spectacle of Edna St. Vincent Millay, a major poet, anguished because she felt denied the right to utter language with clarity, in her own way. One wishes that she had read or reread Henry James's "The Art of Fiction," that excellent statement affirming literary freedom, and decrying most critical rules as nonsense. To "rules" might well be added, "and the current fashion, too."

She looked like a gypsy. She would smile and I would wave. I would drive on to work; she would await her bus for school, an anonymous child I did not know. But because I was sad then, her smile was like the song of the child in Browning's *Pippa Passes*, that changed the lives of people after she had gone by their homes. Years later I learned that she had married and moved to a distant place. Possibly, I wouldn't recognize her now. But I am grateful to that bright little gypsy face and her inspirited morning smile for a man who once, for a time, was adrift in his heart.

PARABLE: At the seacoast low tide rocks appear in morning silhouettes, to remain exposed for what must seem like millennia to certain minute creatures. "Low tide!" cry the Barnacles. "It's the eternal norm. Our forefathers discovered these sea mountains where we the noble Barnacles dwell for all time in the sun."

In the final lull of the outgone tide a Barnacle scientist points a foot at our cabin, saying, "In prehistoric times the waters were up there, because blue mussel shells, homes of the long expired Pelecypods, are said to have been found there. But never again will the great flood rise. We are safe in our permanent status quo of filth and mud."

A Mussel prophet, still alive in a high tide pool, smiles down at the prideful Barnacles. "The drought is brief; soon the Great Tide, created for Mussels, will be back for another billion years."

Still higher on the land a man smiles at the Barnacles and Mussels, knowing himself to be, no matter how he ravages Earth, the only true and permanent species, beloved of Nature.

***

Some people of great gifts, even genius, have postured to the world in quixotic attire, with extravagant manners and speech, and furiously exotic shenanigans. Among such were acidulous James McNeill Whistler, flamboyant Oscar Wilde, over-versatile Jean Cocteau and the self-destructive F. Scott Fitzgerald. Edgar Degas said to Whistler, "You behave as if you had no talent." An old-time schoolteacher once insisted that creative people should behave just like others. But the artist carries a burden—his vision, and if he cries out in pain or wild ecstasy and we do not understand, it is because we cannot see the kind of Host he holds before him.

***

At eleven years of age I snitched an ear of corn from the deacon's field. A chum and I were braving a night in a lean-to camp. We roasted the corn, gloating over our escapade, and I still love burned corn. Rain drove us cravenly to the barn where, crouched in safety, I guiltily feared what the deacon would do if he found out. He never did, or never said, maybe, but as a boy I felt sure that I would face his trembling ghost, the accusatory finger barring me from heaven.

I am not so naive as to suppose that any epoch was ideal. Life is pitiless and lethal from the microcosm upward. Yet we are lost without covenants—not absolutes because we are too ignorant to know if there are any, but we need the dream of the unseen good, the blur of hope beyond the farthermost quasar. O. W. Holmes, Jr., said that we must guide our lives by a star we have never seen. Destroy that: the result is Chaos.

I do a bit of porch repair. Nature is all too ready to pounce upon a human domicile. Once I neglected a vine; it all but devoured the cottage I then occupied. Earth, giver of all things, turns out to be a stern lender. Treat her bounty carelessly, back she seizes it, until even a chimney is hidden in a mound, as any archaeologist knows. We pay not only on the mortgage—the ultimate banker is Nature, who exacts the interest of upkeep, or forecloses with dissolution.

Holy days are pre-established in most religions. We do not invent them. But most of us have private holy days, honored in chapels of memory. One such for me, shared by no one else, was a day when, having permission to "leave the room" as it was delicately called, I stood on a schoolhouse steps. Before me curved a shallow valley attired in ground fog the color of old silver. I knew each path, brook, wood and field of it, but for the moment it was a world of medieval legend. I vowed to remember the day every year, and so I have. The day? Oh, I told the valley I'd keep it a secret. A boy's honor, you know.

Sometimes I wish I could go decades back and counsel my younger self. I'd rise before him like a genie and say gently that he is in part the architect of his problems, that his strong ideas need something else, a looking inward, a confrontation of himself. "You are supposing yourself to be in possession of the whole truth, dear boy," I'd add. But I have no time-machine and cannot go back. The Genie of Hindsight is a rocking-chair philosopher.

❧

When I remember my old swimming hole, I think of a fellow we called "the bully." He was the bad boy who beat up on little kids. I was a little kid. Then in the river one day I was wearing waterwings. They slipped to my heels and I was under, drowning. But I was seized and borne to the bank, rescued by the bully. Years later at a bus stop a meek, small, elderly man called me by name, and we talked of childhood, but he, as is always touching in heroes, could not recall that he had saved my life.

❧

If I too often write in this journal like a gentle soul at peace with itself and life, I console myself that the sweet smile of my venerable face hardens into granite when I go to vote. The *mihi et musis* philosopher conceals a tough old coot who hates corruption, cruelty and the despoiling of the world.

❧

We cannot at all times live on exalted levels. The poet Petrarch wrote noble sonnets to Laura his beloved, yet composed sheer bombast in letters about politics. He longed for spiritual nobility, but dressed like a popinjay.

65

July

This that you now do voluntarily, and do always, and not that other dreamlike aim, is the truth of you. Having agreed with yourself about this, you feel better. An equilibrium establishes itself in your life; you face experience with a new regality and purpose. It is as fine to nurture houseplants, year in and out, as to build bridges over chasms in the Andes.

Brahms complained of the tramp of Beethoven's feet, close behind him. It is so for every artist. In his turn, Beethoven had had to find his way after experiencing the music of Johann Sebastian Bach, whose name, as Beethoven said, meant "brook," but should have been *Meer*, meaning "ocean."

I neared the steps of a store, apprehensive because a little left knee arthritis would make the ascent slightly irksome. Another man, with two canes, was there at the same time. "Steps are kind of rough if you're a bit lame," said I in the empathetic tone of a fellow sufferer. I tapped my knee. He replied, "Got the damn thing all over." I waited to let him slowly precede me, then followed. At the top, far deeper in pain than I, he was holding wide the door for me.

I have no wish to claim that I am as honest as Abe Lincoln who returned a penny or some such sum, walking miles to do it. But two halves of half-pound bacon so stuck together that neither my wife nor I nor the market lady espied them, and we were charged for only one. The next week we reported the oversight, paid the missing sum and were complimented. It was only because we hold that this sort of thing should be in every act however small, as if, like faithful ants, one by one we add a grain to our ideal of society.

In 1641 Nathaniel Ward, who in a serious mood drew up in Massachusetts our first "Body of Liberties," enjoyed poking satiric fun in his book, *The Simple Cobbler*. He liked to invent words, as did Lewis Carroll many years later. "New quoddled words," Ward called them, and he would write cheerfully of "a nugiperous Gentledame" or "the nudiustertian fashion of the Court." Apparently there were foibles in fashions then as now, in England as well as Puritan New England. What a nudiustertian getup might have been is not known, but one cannot be blamed for gentle musings that, even after 333 years, put one into a framistasian quidditude.

I once wrote, "Art is the moment of equilibrium between Apollo and Dionysos," that is, between reason and emotion, discipline and abandon. But the arts, like life, are not so ordered. Many a sonnet is written with sobs, yet is excellent. Many a depiction of the wildest passion is a coolly calculated performance. My pithy saying may have a certain truth, provided it leaves room for the infinite vagaries of the human mind and heart.

In everyday speech we quote bygone authors. If we say that familiarity breeds contempt, that every dog has his day and that so-and-so has a finger in every pie, while a stitch in time saves nine, we quote Cervantes. If we speak of the ship of state, we are using the words of Sophocles. Do you do something in the twinkling of an eye and is money the root of all evil? Both sayings are in the New Testament. If after an evening which you praise as a feast of reason and flow of soul, after which, nonetheless, you could not sleep a wink, you are quoting Alexander Pope's translation of the Satires of Horace.

When young, I was reading hell-bent for final answers to everything. Now I stroll at the library with a foolish grin past metaphysics and the social sciences and sheepishly pick an agreeable biography and a fat volume full of pictures.

Pact With Me: I shall go on observing the world of Man both with happiness and the gravest concern for many aspects of this inhabited planet, but despite that observing, that awareness, that effort to help in any small way, I shall in all this remain my own self, not lost in the hurricane of time and events, unconfused, my values unshattered, as I guard my private reverence for love and respect for every man's faith, and shall go on listening with undiminished ardor to music, to the voice of literature, welcoming the life-enhancement of art and honing all my senses to Nature, as if I were the first to know of such things, and as if, whatever happens, they cannot perish.

Very well, I arise from a primordial molecule and certain conditions stirred it to reproduce. Then what of the atoms in the molecule? Did they arrive at their intricate structure by a mindless jostling of happenchances? Then the same happenchances, dumbly and without purpose, have produced all we know, all we see, from the bright green maple leaf at my window to the farthermost quasar? As a Vermonter used to say, " 'Taint likely."

An elder of our tribe would be wise indeed to stand upon a summit at some later peak of life and say, looking back, "I am content that I have done my best, given the imperfect clay that I am. Without guilt, I regret much; without pride, I approve much."

The sickle moon at dawn is just east of the brilliant Venus. So it will be on this day in a trillion years and likely will be seen by no man. Many scientists now believe there to be innumerable civilizations on planets like ours, throughout our galaxy and every galaxy. At a certain point in a planet's technology (the point where we are now) there perhaps arrives a capability for self-destruction. The planet's creatures choose: extinction or survival. It may matter little to the universe which choice is made. Which reminds me of a verse I wrote in my teens:

> "The Earth collided with a wandering star
> And both in fragments fell and fell forever,
> But to the gods who watched it from afar
> The thing had no significance whatever."

—I wonder how we'll choose.

69

There are certain people I've always loved to see, although some are not now living. They are the walkers. One—a man with a blithesome Irish face, all smile. Another—a tiny aged lady, quick as a hummingbird, cussing softly while picking up litter. Then—an old musician, limping with his cane, bound half a mile to the library. And one like a Roman senator, in his eighties, bareheaded in all seasons, passing my house every morning.

To cull bits from journals present and past, as I do these days, is both rewarding and dismaying. Did I really once think so and so? Or, what inspired that feverish rhetoric? Or, come, lad, was that not an unbecoming day of bitterness, when now as your elder I feel no such emotion? Then, here and there, that callow fellow, a mere upstart, said something better than I now might. And back there, how serious we were, my friend, never revealing that we could cut a caper or two or lift that left eyebrow with a Satanic and fetching bit of humor.

Nowadays as a creature of habit I make my morning coffee, light a pipe and sit down to write, all in a precise sequence. I go the same routes to the Square or market like an ant inexorably following its invisible highway. Once I did the same, going to and from work. But I make a promise—tomorrow I'll try a cup other than my pet coffee mug, and vary the route to market and Square. I'll take a stroll north instead of east, and south, not west. For who knows, there may be a whole new world, even El Dorado, just around an untried corner.

In 1630 William Bradford, second governor of "Plimoth Plantation" as he called it, wrote its history, "*The which,*" he said, "*I shall endevor to manifest in a plaine stile, with singuler regard unto ye simple trueth in all things, at least as near as my slender judgmente can attaine the same.*" Now methinks it woulde be seemlie of all who are now here so many longe generations since, to plunge our mindes into heartfelt meditation and selfe-examination, to determine yet again our rootes, and thereon ponder deeply, for onlie by so doing may we eternally cherish all that we came here for and so protect it and the trueth that is in our hearts.

In a letter I wrote while in the sixth grade I said that I was allowed to go barefoot and "didn't hurt my feet either, except a nail in my foot, cut shin, stubbed toe, and bleeding nose. Hum, not much." Well, "blessings on thee, barefoot boy," and I see you liked commas even then!

In youth the passionate focus of my life was cityward. The metropolis was a golden ingot at the heart of civilization. But Place is a state of mind. Now I would not exchange this view of Colonial homes, trees and shrubs and nearby hills for all the shining peaks of megalopolis. But I know that others joyfully flee their bucolic homes for city apartments. We are like magnetic needles, whose north has unpredictable ways of changing its position.

At their most subtle, dawns are powder blue lines across a Venetian blind in my study, like those on a student's writing pad. My

71

dawn collection, which is beyond price and not for sale, yields innumerable treasures, a gamut from the subtle to processions of giant clouds, dark and regal, coursing with ominous haste and power above the morning hills, reminding me of Valhalla or the Beethoven Fourth Piano Concerto in which tiny Man, uttering a quiet melody on the piano against the orchestra, seems to defy the magnitude of forces that seek to overwhelm him.

Once I toted home a curious broken brick to my parents, earnestly announcing that I had found a relic of a lost civilization, an American Nineveh. I was not laughed at, and was advised to keep it in my room as perhaps a rare treasure. It is long lost, and now I suppose it to have been from a tumbled chimney, buried in a roadside bank. Well, it might have dated from Revolutionary times, as did our house, and that is Nineveh enough for me.

August

What admonitions are given us by homes of the great. "We are, you observe," they tell us, "only such dwellings as you have also known, only such ordinary materials as you have seen and touched. Yet, think, what was perceived here by those you have come to honor." So speak the small bare room in Pittsfield, Massachusetts, where Herman Melville wrestled with *Moby Dick*, that other in Salem, Massachusetts, where Nathaniel Hawthorne's *The Scarlet Letter* was born, and the bedroom in Amherst, Massachusetts, where Emily Dickinson had heard no news but "bulletins all day from Immortality." As for that hut and pond and the height of thought he brought there, Henry David Thoreau, as we visit the cairn of stones at the site, facing the sunlit water, well might shake his ghostly head at our narrow vision. Do we not know, he seems to say, that every pond is Walden?

Music, love of which has been a major part of my life, has brought me some of my dearest friendships. Even in small ways it unexpectedly opens doors. I was in a proofroom consulting a dictionary. The sole proofreader, a distinguished elderly lady, her back to me, was whistling a passage from a Beethoven piano sonata.

As she neared the end of a phrase I finished it for her. "You too?" she said softly. That was all, but it is a cherished memory of my professional editing career. The music? Sonata No. 13, the Adagio in A major.

※

While being X-rayed and otherwise checked out, I was impressed with the skill, intelligence and courtesy of the clinic and hospital staff. Throughout a process not soothing to one's dignity, they somehow preserved it. More than radiology must be in their training, and this is to link one of the humanities with science. It is a linkage without which any science is barren, but with it almost divine.

※

In my teens I was obsessed with *Hamlet*. Later I was just as fond of Shakespeare's jesters, like Touchstone in *As You Like It*. I own a charming steel engraving of him as he twits and woos the "country wench" Audrey, as she is called in the *dramatis personae*. Growing up would have been easier had I let those madcap sages fill me as much with the comic spirit as did *Hamlet* characters with tragedy, for laughter is as profound as tears, telling us that sometimes the play leads on to rare delights when life, now and then, behaves itself.

※

I understand my fellowman and shall not quarrel with him because, poor souls, we are one day to become only memories in the disappearing century. Let us pass the time in peace.

74

There are times when I open some excellent book, even a great one, and give up, aware that I am reading through a mist of inattention. Those are the days when the world so fills me that the book seems not to relate to the formidable present. We lack the ease of a long, "deep-breathed" era as the writer John Cowper Powys called such a time. Doubtless that ease was illusion, ignorance of deep workings in society. It left us at the birth of nuclear fission when, as Prospero says in *The Tempest*,

> "Our revels are now ended. These our actors,
> As I foretold you, were all spirits, and
> Are melted into air, into thin air."

Yet at other times great works by great minds all but ascend from the page with enduring authority, and it is then that I know what we live by. The dusty book becomes a fount, replenishing the drought of our age, affirming that if we so will it there may still be time to make a masterpiece of Earth.

The stage was empty, the curtain up. Saint-Saëns' *The Swan* began. A king rose to his feet, as did his queen—Albert and Elizabeth of Belgium. The audience also rose. Anna Pavlova had died the day before.

If I am correct, these weakening August crickets are playing spiccato quarter notes, a single tone, F sharp in the third octave above middle C. A long cry, musically, from the virtuosity of the first robin. A cricket is like a buoy far out in a bay, its lessening monosyllable tolling of coming winter.

We are all nostalgic, I as much as any. It expresses our aversion to this violent age. Yet I caution myself. Before me is a reproduction of a sixteenth-century painting, a tranquil landscape, sporting children, gentle mothers and the king going by in his elegance. I remind myself that the sporting children often died young; the angler had a short life expectancy; childbirth slew many women; the king could have a dissenter burned; surgery was agony; and disease unchecked. I sigh at the halcyon landscape that has for a moment deceived me, and look out at my own world with a better heart.

❦

We go to a private, tiny art exhibit in a country manse. Everything about the place has an air of ruined gentility on the verge of cheery insanity. As we tiptoe out an aged lady careens down the drive, madly flapping her hands in farewell. A ruddy, grinning old boy passes us, lugging a gallon of gin and crying, "What a *mahvelous* day!" A whole Gothic novel in this.

❦

I leaf through old book review magazines and newspapers. When young I read them avidly to learn the language of the sophisticates. I was in a hurry to acquire what I esteemed was savoir-faire. In maturity I am not concerned to be an "in" person, or to keep up with what is regarded as "in" from hour to hour. Even my slang is mellowed with outdatedness, and I don't propose to change to its later equivalents. One earns the right to be unfashionable and perhaps a bit perversely quaint.

76

Words associated with what we love have their own look of particular beauty. I have loved typography as an editor. To me, there is enchantment in names of typefaces, like Cheltenham, Goudy, Garamond, Baskerville, Bodoni, Benedictine and many others. I've loved music. The very words adagio, andante, allegro, grazioso, espressivo and others evoke remembered musical passages. Years ago I read critics with staring fascination, as such terms all but sounded for me concerts I had not heard. It must be so of anything one cherishes, whether it is the gardener's mulch, the gourmet's pot, the tools of the hobbyist. In this respect where there is meaning everything possesses intrinsic grace and magic.

I read a bitter novel. Everything is ugly, cruel. I turn to a TV story of a loving family in an ideal rural setting. All is goodness to the point of saccharinity. Which is true? The pessimist nurtures a secret Eden as extreme as the present reality he hates. The optimist is a hater, too, hating the cruel and ugly, and recognizing only the bright and beautiful. But Life is too restive to sit for its portrait, and will not be finally stated as this or that.

A lovely lady phones me from California. Her charming voice takes me back to spring freshets, meadows and woodlands, to the first mayflowers, to the fragrance of mowing, to the stories we enacted of our own conjuring. Was she then my childhood sweetheart, remembering me after all the years? In a most spiritual sense, yes, and I closed my eyes, hearing again the spoken words of one who wandered with me on adventures of such

77

derring-do, like those of Robert Louis Stevenson's *A Child's Garden of Verses*—my first kid sister.

❦

The small sign was affixed to a houseboat, moored in a cove. Whenever I passed that way I looked for it with affection. I read, "*MULTUM IN PARVO*," which I suspect was faultier Latin than my own. "Much in Little." It made me think of the simple materials of all the men and women who from humble starts and places nonetheless have contributed to the values and conscience of mankind.

❦

So the scrawny princess married the homely prince and they lived happily ever after. That's not how the story goes, but it is often the way life goes. Few are beauties, male or female, and then not for long. I was struck by this in a supermarket. There was something familiar in all the faces and figures, a common denominator, a reassuring absence of stunning good looks. "People," I thought, "aren't heroes and heroines. In real life they're character actors." As if in confirmation, a glass door reflection showed me a gaunt old fellow in an out-of-date gray jacket, baggy maroon slacks and battered shoes. He was walking with slow care, and his effort at a pale smile seemed more like a wince of pain or fatigue. "Proves my point," flashed my mind— and then I recognized myself.

❦

We cannot prevent catastrophe or normal death, but for the rest of human suffering we have the powerful tools of intelli-

gence and compassion, although both go awry and lapse a fright-
ful percentage of the time. But they are all we have: think, have
pity, act. The principle engirdles the Earth.

※※

I watch a parade. It has passed this way for twenty-six years of
my life here. Only the personnel has changed, largely. There
were children then whose own children now march by. The
school band uniforms, bright and dashing, seemed unchanged,
and I wondered how many, now grown up, had worn them.
For a parade, in itself the same yet never the same from year to
year, is like the immortality of the genes, the race, the life-river
that is a constant although we yield our immediate roles to
others, and those to still others.

※※

With insensate ruthlessness man in wartime destroys what his
own hands have created in his intervals of sanity. Such have been
the Parthenon, the cathedrals of Rheims and Rouen, the noble
architecture of Coventry and Monte Cassino. Man is a split creature, archangelic and diabolic. His saving grace is that his better
side keeps trying. In this he is at least not like animals that toy
with prey, as if torture were an amusingly necessary part of the
kill. Nature has been worse than blind there. She has a strange
two-sidedness, which we inherit and hope to amend. In our garden this year we amended nature. A Japanese tree peony began
to flower—a single treasure of beauty. With deadly accuracy a
pigeon left its mark in the blossom. We washed nature's wit-
ticism to the base, where it will serve better as nitrogen. For the
moment, nature is a little less schizophrenic and we are on the
side of the angels.

79

Stage fright is nothing to be ashamed of. The late Pablo Casals, considered by many the world's greatest violincellist, never got over it. In his nineties he said, "The thought of a public performance is still a nightmare."

Just as painters work in various media, oil, watercolor and so forth, so a writer works in a medium, that of expressing experience in words. His materials include the dilemmas of his own life, his times, his genetic heritage, his hectic or organized papers. As if adrift in a dinghy, he rows his course in a complex and agitated sea, but with the difference that although a sea has shores, his mind ought to be shoreless.

Midsummer and a day of beauty, the sky clear, the vegetable plot a living symbol of fertility, grass maturely green, flowers still arriving as if for town meeting and happy worms becoming protein in happier birds. All things are getting on quite well without me, and I doubt that Nature, just there below my porch, is noticing that I am standing there, watching.

A bird flies back and forth, very upset. He utters short jabbing squawks. Another cheeps excitedly. It seems to be a territorial dispute, cheep versus squawk. The issue, it appears, is the maple at my study window. Some point of bird international law is at stake. I cannot tell which is the aggressor, which the victim. But now they have quieted. Peace, at least for the moment, has come, probably no more just and honorable a peace than any in history.

In the fourth century B.C. Greece was in her first stage of decline, despite the presence of Plato, Aristotle, Isocrates, Demosthenes and Menander. Much of what happened applies with terrible warning to our own time. Noble Greek democracy, a symbol of every man's freedom, except for its slaves, became corrupt. Plato and Aristotle withdrew from the mess; Isocrates pleaded in vain for peace and equality; Demosthenes killed himself; and Menander wrote to please an elite society. Then a long silence—until sober-minded Plutarch wrote the epitaph of Greece.

AUTUMN

September

If as we grow older we can look back without rancor, that is, with understanding, forgiveness and self-forgiving, we have nurtured and brought to flower one of the greatest arts of life.

I deeply admire Virginia Woolf as a novelist, but cannot abide her when she writes of George Eliot, ". . . the culture, the philosophy, the fame and the influence were all built upon a very humble foundation—she was the granddaughter of a carpenter." Did Mrs. Woolf suppose that her knighted Stephen forebears had not themselves descended from the exceedingly more humble and indeed savage foundations of England's dawn?

Transported to any epoch we might feel quite at home. In the agora, marketplace of antique Athens, we'd be on familiar ground, glumly paying our obols for overpriced produce, and the sight of Pericles and his brilliant mistress Aspasia doing the same would not sweeten our mood. In Chaucer's time we could greet every Canterbury pilgrim as a neighbor. Lift us to the future and some galactic civilization and we might sit down to an outer space cocktail with an agreeable monster and be comparing photos of our homefolks.

A friend once said that in my study one might see, over there, a letter dated 1916, over here another dated 1920, another 1939. I glance about. Yes, here is a 1916 letter to me from the minister's wife, Mrs. T. Edward Davies, of Westminster, Connecticut. She quotes Thomas Henry Huxley: "The most important part of all education is to make yourself do what you should do, when you should do it, whether you like it or not." I find a 1921 letter. In that summer I was a New York *World* office boy, in the art department. I wanted to be a cartoonist. I wrote blithely to my mother, who had once been on the paper, that I was "meeting all kinds of corking people, Ralph Pulitzer, Herbert Bayard Swope, and such guys." Bless 'em, they hired me as a cub later on.

✶✶

On FM I hear medieval church music. How desperately needful it is not to disbelieve in beauty and in every other excellent value of life, despite the horrors man commits.

✶✶

I am pronounced in good shape by my doctor. But the world is still a realm of suffering, and this fills me with the pity and awe of old Greek tragedy. I for the present know joy; others, agony.

✶✶

It is my habit to welcome the noble qualities of life as if, in the dark forest of the world's sorrows, I permit myself to reach out into rays of light. On occasion people express in words and acts an awesome ideality. Recently I have seen several in a ceremony

86

of a faith not mine, as they spoke of it on a hilltop. And I have seen a person, now for long bereaved, sublime in her love and belief that she will be joined again with her beloved. I have looked at a group of my own dear ones, seeing almost more beauty and love than a man can bear. Then as my hands gather rays like these I recall a bit of *Genesis*, "Behold, this dreamer cometh," and I can well believe that these mysteries and aspirations abiding deep in human natures comprise the hope of our existence.

⁂

A spider is on the window. I get a jar and card, my way of returning creatures to nature if they are harmless. But he crawls into a crack. I lower the sash, hoping not to crush him. In an hour he is out, healthy. I pick up the jar and card, but the idiot disappears again. I pray to the spirit who watches over stupid spiders. "Tell him," I suggest, "that he is in the presence of a strange phenomenon—mercy."

The spider seems to have heard. He emerges, I capture him and out he goes onto a bush. I am content, the spider is free and I compliment the spirit who whispered to him. It pleases me that we, all three, now have an amiable morning.

⁂

A schoolboy passes my house, exclaiming, as if describing an unimaginable antiquity, "She's about thirty-two years old!"

⁂

Dear Posterity: While I have an excellent head for budgeting and forecasting future income and outgo, I sometimes err in

87

arithmetic. I forecast an ominous deficit for the summer, only to find a small surplus. I therefore recommend that you never despair (*nil desperandum* is our family motto), since time is a stream and money the mere foam thereon.

❧

There is no pornography in the vegetable kingdom. A bright red rosebush this summer for weeks displayed its naked allure with the utmost abandon and charm and no officers hustled it into a patrol car.

❧

When I find myself, reading with a superior smile about medieval doctors who diagnosed ailments as "humours," or the incorrect guesses about atoms in Lucretius' time (about 55 B.C.), or grin at pathetic ancient maps of the known world, I reflect that most of archaeology now must be rewritten because of the discovery of radiocarbon dating combined with tree ring calibration. History as we learned it is cockeyed, in vast areas.

❧

Out of my papers pops a single sheet of rules for my brother, a sister (another sister was still a baby and others were not yet born) and me. I am four. The rules: Don't argue. Don't talk when older people are talking. Mind mother the first time that she speaks. Pick up things you drop. Don't say vulgar words. Don't call names. Be honorable, truthful and generous. Don't hang on the front gate. Our names are signed in our mother's distinguished handwriting.

88

I still do fairly well with the rules, even though she is not here to judge. I can't be too sure of the vulgar words, but time and usage have changed their impact. Also, I have no gate or I might just, as a playful grandfather, hang on it for the hell of it.

※

Recently I attained a year that disproved a notion of many years, that the one just before it would do me in. It was based on the mean between the deaths of my parents—the guess of some ass of a pundit long ago. Sheer nonsense. We are only partly the product of parents; a multitude of ancestors preceded them. Besides, by some mysterious shake of the genetic dice, we are ourselves, and beyond this our times differ, with fabulous medical techniques that would have seemed like witchcraft to our fore-bears.

※

When I was a bit overweight I noted with satisfaction that many a man looks distinguished if his belly bulges. Now that I am rather underweight I observe how spruce and alert seem the gentlemen I pass, whose belts most probably have as many new holes as mine.

※

Not since the eighteenth century have people in this country been so concerned about the principles upon which our society was founded. Political philosophers from the sixteenth through the eighteenth centuries speak to us now with new force. The question then as now was, Wherein lies sovereignty? Surely a nation is not sick if, as has happened not only with justices but

89

with plain and earnest people who perhaps read little ordinarily, millions have scanned the Constitution as if it were a love letter.

⁂

Not even the greatest know if their fame will endure. John Keats wrote, "Here lies one whose name was writ in water." Montaigne said, "What I do, it is but bungling and wants both polishing and beauty." We all plod incognito in our ways, and out of hordes of us a few are remembered. But is it so poor a fate to be unnamed, yet to have left behind us, unwittingly, some one lasting touch of inspiration, as did the writers over a thousand years of the Psalms which, though partly attributed to David, were mostly anonymous?

⁂

Addicted as I am to what is called macabre Yankee humor, I often describe myself as a wan ancient seen doddering about, smiling at babies, feeding pigeons and hailing beauteous Nature. All a lie. Wan I am but I dodder not, and sometimes I direct a tolerant wince at a tot (always remembering the population explosion). As for pigeons, in a bad winter they might get a few sunflower seeds from me. But by and large, within my meek outward aspect is a lion who is apt to stare down a baby, shoo a pigeon and tell Nature to go to the devil.

⁂

Sometimes I look at the title of this journal and feel that I should say something about Mount Monadnock. But it is as frustrating to commend a mountain as it is to pat an ocean. A mountain is a flighty sort, with a theatrical flair for dressing up. One day it is bland and ingenuous, as if saying with Touchstone in *As You Like It*, "Doth my simple feature content you?"

Next day it is a King Lear with a mad crown of storm. I prefer, anyway, to look at a mountain from afar with my mouth soundlessly open. It doesn't need my praise, no, nor my hard-boiled eggshells and beer cans ground with my heels onto its face.

Given its choice, the poor dumb monster just wants, most likely, to be what it is, without my loud hosannas.

✥

A book, for me, is likely to become ten books, hauled forth for reference. I read Emerson's 1833 visit to Carlyle, Coleridge and Wordsworth and presently sit in a heap of books, like a chipmunk on a woodpile. I learn that Coleridge spilled snuff on his waistcoat, and so I look up snuff. Carlyle is described as playful and humorous, but I must at once verify what Margaret Fuller Ossoli thought of him—that he rushed upon one like "a torrent of sound." Amusing to find anyone outtalking Margaret.

Then I read that Wordsworth recited to Emerson three sonnets he had written about Fingal's Cave. Promptly I find them, but am deflected as I recall the Fingal's Cave Overture of Mendelssohn, and I forget books and delve into my ungodly tattered stack of music. But perhaps this is what reading is all about—to set up in us a chain reaction.

✥

I advise a man, drawing upon my personal experience, and then, as he goes along with a higher heart, I begin to wonder. The first lesson of semantics is that A is not B. My life is not his life. Using my advice he may fall on his face. I am resolved to cultivate a more skeptical modesty and be careful how I try to clarify life for others.

Once with confusion in my heart I misjudged an entire family, only to learn years later that all had thought well of me.

October

Sounds: I do not care for incessant barking, the yawps of angry bluejays, the growls of cats in confrontation, the screech of cars at my corner. I prefer the boy who goes by singing, the man who whistles quite musically as he passes, the summer-long melody of the old robin in the silver maple. The most heartrending sound recently was that of a very small boy who tripped. His bag of food, almost bigger than himself, had spilled into the gutter, torn asunder, milk flowing, eggs a white and yellow mess, tomatoes rolling into the drain. Helpless, he just lay flat, blasted by total disaster, and then, piteously, more prayer than blasphemy, he sobbed, "Jee–sus Christ."

I have written book, play and music criticism, but have always been too much in sympathy with the labors of these to be of much constructive help. At firsthand I know what it is to write, to study music and, by proxy, to act because I descend from generations of a theatre family. A good critic needs this empathy, yet should stand apart with a mind possessing "a certain largeness" as the English writer John Morley in part defined literature.

The good critic is not a nitpicker; he is perhaps more like the cool light slanting into the studio, illuminating the modeled contours of sculpture for our better understanding.

Long ago a young architect rang my doorbell at midnight. He was wild-eyed, distraught. His world had crashed. It came out that his teacher, a famed architect, had drilled into him the dictum "Form follows function." No creative frills, only grim usefulness. But he had visited his mentor's home, and seeing a fine window on a wall had asked its function. "Oh, it just looks good there," said his teacher. I gave my distracted friend a stiff shot of shamelessly aesthetic booze.

❦

Seacoast note: An ocean is so authoritative; to feel important a fishing cove must busy itself night and day.

❦

At the ocean one comes to see eternal water, to listen, acknowledge its presence and to remember that the first settlers crossed this very body. This is Europe, as it were, reaching forth, ending here. We observe a force not that of man, whose lesser works must be oriented to it with lighthouses, seafood and tourist knicknacks. I make only simple notes and sketches. Philosophy is for inland groves; ocean is its own philosophy.

❦

The coastal day "commences," as the old whaling logs would say, in pastel tones and the red dagger of sunrise. A ship with a tall mast bears east, into a perspective of tranquil pink that blends into the sky. It is hard to believe that beyond the horizon are large sophisticated fishing vessels of other countries, some with intricate electronic gear monitoring us, as we monitor them in turn. A grim watching game goes on, and the Down East fishermen are being ruined by the huge catches of the larger craft.

94

As we come late to our rented cottage overlooking the shore a lady who is a guest in the next house greets us in the dark:

"What do you think?" Her accent is French and deep.

Profound query. I decide upon a simple reply. "It is very nice," I say.

"Have a good dream." Then, after a pause, "Not bad."

She goes indoors like a sea goddess entering a temple. I reflect that I might have answered, "*C'est très plaisant mais la mer est un petit froide*," but my school French had given me no ready conversation. It taught me to say, "The suitcase of my grandfather is not on the train," which would be incomprehensible to a daughter of Neptune. The exchange might have gone:

"What do you think?" Neighborly like.

"*Ah, madame, nous pensons que—*" Stuck. My wife and I look falteringly at each other.

"Have a good dream."

"*Mais oui, madame, et nous espérons que vous—*" m–m, what is dream? *Songez bien*? Probably not. Hours later I remember "*rêve*" with the upside down "v" on the first "e." Days later I look up "*Songez bien.*" It would have been O.K.

"Not bad."

"*Oui, pas mal.*" But Persephone or Thetis or whoever she was has gone and, what do you think, we have a good dream, not bad.

Autumn days more resemble duration than time—the flow of living that we feel, not the goosestep of the clock. Duration is as mysterious as thought. Had neither clock nor calendar been invented we should still have our sense of this measureless experience, as unmarked as it must be in the consciousness of every other kind of creature. To peer into what eternity may be, stroll from a room where the clock ticks, into one lacking that instrument, and shut the door and look slowly around in silence. It is a realm of beauty.

Sudden winds raid the trees, architecture of summer. Leaves rush like war refugees, and late at night the victor pounds his chest with a bellow of thunder, like a Minotaur in the earth. Today the stripped foliage concedes the season, ravished by the monster. I find a last earwig in the bathtub and consign him to the sewer, I, another monster, annihilating summer.

Soon we shall have the aspect of winter, the musing gray of distance through the leaf-lorn branches, the vaporous sky of the Angles and Jutes facing the North Sea in the age of Beowulf.

I feel like an ancient Saxon harpist, singing the suffering and joy of men and women, speaking of life and time and dying, and what is lovely, just and true. Meanwhile, like one of the Fates, the East wind divides the gray clouds and stitches them together again, with impersonal repetition.

But it's the month of Hallowe'en and "behold, a troop cometh." We always especially praise those who have devised their own costumes and makeup, and I am fondest of the smallest, urged to trick or treat for the first time by a nearby mother in the shadows, some tot no bigger than a minute, braving the very door of the giant.

This autumn morning I can think of nothing to set down in my journal. No? Wait . . . I fly above my life. Down there is the

Connecticut village of my boyhood, church, school, brook and meadow. Now I am over Brooklyn, New York, watching a serious kid on a bike, with Maeterlinck in his pocket. I am over Greenwich Village, seeing myself walking with a girl. Their whispering pursues me. I wing across America and am on a white ferry scudded by seagulls near the Golden Gate. At long last in New England there is sunshine on a green shore, and a dark-eyed woman and I are speaking of love. Not a bad mental harvest for an Autumn dawn.

❦

A beloved friend, a Greek artist, exclaims to me, "Archimedes, Socrates, Pythagoras, Beethoven—all dead. And I am still alive! How is this?" (I wrote this in my journal thirty years ago. Last week he phoned me, long distance, with no loss of that wonderful vigor.)

❦

From the same year: Trying to arrange my activities—writing, reading, study, music, budgeting, letters, bathing, house care, filing. I have no idea what was being studied, or why a special note about bathing was needed. As for the rest, ah me, they're still not "arranged."

❦

Again, back there: A writer is drafted and tells me, "I am to be living instead of writing the end of my novel." (He survived the war.)

And this: My Greek friend and I, fellow workers in a wartime shipyard, stand on the bridge of a Liberty ship. We look out over miles of steel, ships in all stages of construction, prefab platforms, whole sections of vessels suspended between giant cranes —five yards, 90,000 people who at change of shift move in rivers out of this vast inferno.

"Look!" cries my philosophic friend. "What ingenuity Man expends on his own destruction!"

✼

Also (I am reminiscent today): I read *A Tale of Two Cities* to my daughter. She seems not to find it too old for her. I'm impressed with the leisurely pace of descriptions. Dickens was bound he would depict a scene if it took the reader the whole century to read it through—a commendable attitude for a writer. We are much too hurried in this rapid and frenzied time.

✼

Just after World War II: At a San Francisco art gallery I look long at photos of art and architecture in Italy, destroyed, pulverized by Axis and Allied bombings—great frescoes by Andrea Mantegna in the Eremitani Church in Padua, blown to bits, unrestorable. Only a soldier's head, in one fresco. There is left, in this one, the most famous of the Early Renaissance frescoes, only a warrior's face—with no brain above it.

✼

Back to now. That was all so long ago. It sets me to thinking about time. I go to our kitchen door, which has a window in its upper part. The rising sun exactly caps the ell chimney of a neighbor. I feel an eerie atavistic thrilling in my spine, then realize that this is an astronomical moment known when Stonehenge was built. In my bathrobe I might be clad in a ceremonial vestment of centuries past, and I feel as if some ancient ghost had reached through aeons to touch my forehead, as if to tell me, "You too are Stonehenge Man."

✶

Poets, novelists and artists have often fled the United States to live in Europe. They have felt the lack here of a long-continued tradition—centuries, even millennia of history, arts and architectures. Thomas Hardy could write of soldiers of Hadrian's time, buried in Roman England. To be sure we don't have that. We do not link up ethnically with Indian origins in America, although we very well may if we think around the world to their Asiatic beginnings. I never look outdoors at just before dawn, say, at ground fog, without reflecting that deep below this house may be their old campfires, and below those the remains of prehistoric Man, older perhaps than those anywhere else, since America is geologically the oldest continent. For some, that is tradition aplenty.

✶

Desperately shy of public speaking, a trait not conquered until I was past forty, I once asked my mother how she could address groups with such ease. She said she had decided, about her own shyness, that everyone was shy, every person in the audience.

✶

The white-clapboarded garage of a neighbor is the terminus of a portion of our garden. One day I saw two little boys practicing

99

the ancient art of graffiti—writing something there. As a child I had done it, when shocking words were new and interesting. So I strolled over and said mildly: "A very nice lady lives there and she might be unhappy if you write things on her wall. Maybe you won't any more, eh?" They agreed and left. I bent low to inspect what innocent foulness they had perpetrated. I disguise their names; they had scrawled: Joey 7, Billy 6.

A Greek friend revisiting his country interceded in some trouble on a bus and was told by the driver and an official that it was none of his business. "Justice and humanity are my business," said the visitor, "the birthright of every Greek since Homer."

I recognize no form of aristocracy. If its imagined superiority is based upon wealth, I think of the Greek philosopher Epictetus who said that he was richer in his one poor cloak than the passing emperor in all his panoply. If based upon lineage, the merest ghetto waif possesses that. If it sets itself up in mansions, clubs or other private enclaves I laugh at its narrow folly and, raising my hands to the stars, say that all this is the enclave of Everyman.

November

Writers often envy literary styles unlike their own. James Gibbons Huneker in his *Chopin* tried an academic style, the least like his own of all his work. Robert Louis Stevenson, who wrote with fluidity and grace, admired Thomas Hardy whose way of writing, said Hardy's second wife, was a "dear dullness." The late critic Carl Van Doren, dispassionate and kindly, was attracted to the fury and venom of Jonathan Swift and wrote a book about him.

Long ago I served a choice sauterne to a European friend at dinner. Gourmet and linguist, with a pirate's voice, he demanded where I had bought the wine and marshaled me to the store, where he denounced the proprietor in four languages for selling such stuff to his friend.

The wine seller insisted that it came from a certain hill behind Paris, a celebrated vintage not far from the slopes of Montmartre. "That hill!" roared my guest. "I know it! Pigs on it!" The wine was exchanged for another, his choice, and we returned to our dinner, my wild gourmet now calm, extolling the red vino he had gotten.

No gourmet, it tasted to me like any table wine, and I thought with poignancy of the despised swine, grunting among ancient grapevines near the Quartier Latin.

High above the sidewalk I hear a squeaky chittering, like scissors needing oil. I look and count nineteen swallows speeding clockwise. Their nervous discussion appears to be of some moment. Finally a consensus is reached, the curving line straightens and the one in front is followed, but I am unsure whether he has been elected leader or is being drummed out of town.

In female sectors of department stores, I, an inadvertent intruder, always take care to be polite to fashion dummies. If I brush such a creature I say, "Sorry." This I do promptly, hoping that it is not alive, since I have always been, I trust, a discreet sophisticate in such matters. Most appalling of all is to nudge accidentally a form conceivable only on some distant planet inhabited by upside down anthropomorphic crustaceans—a pair of pantyhosed legs aimed ceilingward like a "V" for Victory gesture, and in my bemusement I have said, "Sorry" to a pink plastic rump.

Everyone has eyries of the spirit, for the shutting out of the world's din. Mine may be a page of Mozart, writing, a book, a bit of clay (although I rarely model nowadays). An old friend, now dead, began each day by going to his front door to look at the field and woods, and he could get in his car in peace, starting to work, if he had espied a tufted titmouse.

My children, grandchildren, nieces, nephews and friends know, possibly to their secret boredom, that when they visit me I am likely to hold a Treasure Hunt. This means getting out files of miscellanies, largely about me. They are spread on the floor and disgorge (I pick one file at random) an architect's idea of what ancient Mycenae looked like; a letter from a sister when little; a postcard of Amos Bronson Alcott's School of Philosophy in Concord, Massachusetts; a Christmas card from an old flame; a letter from a freighter's first mate, from Singapore; a cartoon by me of a bearded violinist, his beard entangled with his bow and fiddle; a Boston Athenaeum ticket entitling me to take out books long ago; a sketch I did of my father listening to a crystal radio set I'd built in 1925; a bit of my teenage rhetoric about spring and summer; a Depression food list (apples 8 cents, eggs 9 cents, corned beef 9 cents). I won't go on—it would take all day. In some way that I cannot define, they are all mementos of my life, its brick and mortar. Archaeology is in part aided by broken shards of excavated sites; perhaps these, perishable though they are, are shards, as are such oddities in anyone's life.

The tender understanding that is possible in people is touchingly expressed in *Close to Colette*, by Maurice Goudeket, the last husband of that great and beloved author. The book is an antidote for our embittered epithet of "chauvinism" this and that. A sonnet by the poet George Sterling ended, "Love is somehow the answer to it all." I know few better truths for the ills of mankind.

Dawn comes like a ghost of remembered mornings. The white hydrangea there—yes, I recall it from yesterday. Slowly grass reminds me that it is green. I see heavy forms becoming trees. Memory by memory the world appears again and as I stretch and yawn in the rising light I begin to remember myself, a bit here, a bit there, and then the rest.

Earth—a strange word descending from Germanic tongues. Uncapitalized it is the stuff we walk on, out of which we and almost everything around us spring. Given a capital E, it is that Earth of the moon shot photos, a planet far away, lighted in black space by the sun, this our Earth where the mites that we are embroil ourselves in troubles or, so versatile are we, sometimes have dreams of divinity.

People say to artists, "I'd like to draw but I can't draw a straight line." If I were an artist I'd tell them, do you see any straight lines in Nature? Then let your lines curve, wriggle, dance, be phantoms of your imagination. If you want a straight line, get a ruler; if you want art, look hard at the letter "S." To William Hogarth (1697–1764), the English painter and engraver, that double curve was what he called "the line of Beauty."

Two ghosts, a pessimist and an optimist, meet on the other side. "See," cries the optimist, "I told you there'd be eternity." "Yes," groans the pessimist, "but it's going to be damned boring."

"I am," a lady in her eighties wrote to me, "exactly the same girl, deep inside me, that I was at fifteen." I wrote back, "Of course!" For what indeed changes in us? Nothing—nothing that has ever had worth and value, nothing that was and is the very centrosome of our personalities.

Know this and we see a bonny lad or lass in the face of every aged person, and in time we may easily prove it in our own mirrors.

As with paintings, there have been literary hoaxes. A legendary third-century A.D. Celtic poet, Ossian, was "translated" by James MacPherson in the eighteenth century—poetry of a high order. MacPherson went on to Parliament and a good income and died unbelieved but undishonored. Another hoaxer of the same century came to a tragic end—Thomas Chatterton of England, a boy of astounding imagination and poetic power. He kept "discovering" fifteenth-century manuscripts which he himself wrote in the antiquated English of that time. At seventeen he committed suicide in an attic while starving. Shelley, Keats and Coleridge hailed his genius, and a monument, albeit rather moralistic, was put up in his memory in Bristol, England.

A rusty wire gate was in place at a corner of our lot when we bought our house. Whether it was there to stop children from going crosslots, I don't know. Envisioning their ancestors using that natural right of way for kids, we dismantled the gate, and the timeless procession goes on. In more than a decade there has been only one incident, when three croci and one lonely tulip were swiped, our prized and meagre emblems of the season. Hardly enough to restore a rusted gate. After all, the unknown moppet had shown good if a bit churlish taste, a curious mixture not limited to beautiful children.

✣

We see our lives as moving and changing from day to day, a calendar progression. We know that this motion and change can be interrupted by happenchance for good or ill. What we are not prepared for is the emergence, from a casual fact or encounter in the depths of our years, of something of major importance, changing our course entirely. It is as if an ember wakes into fire, or an island surfaces where one had not been. Out of the past a voice greets us, long-delayed mail arrives, the phone rings, and we are presently out upon some new plateau of destiny. This is the very stuff of old-time fiction, and when it is true in real life it comes like a visitor bearing credentials of magic—again, for good or ill.

✣

I think that I am secretly fond of November. It is maligned as a time of melancholy. The year has become as silent as a stilled cricket. Color has muted to distant purples. We don mental moccasins as if, far within, we were aborigines like those who long ago preceded us in these dawns and twilights. True, the harvest festival is to come, when uncles loosen their belts and holiday accidents redden the land, but until then we are in a hushed and reverent world of cornstalks and amethystine tranquillity.

106

What children casually know nowadays! Kids of my time would be mental pigmies if set beside them. One evening I was referring in adult conversation to the Boston Symphony. I groped for the last name of the musical director after I had given his first, "Seijii—" My ten-year-old granddaughter, toying with a puppet, coolly helped: "Ozawa."

✣

Wonder what a bee does on a rainy day? A shrub outside, thick with blossoms, one day, was alive with bees. The next day not one. Do they huddle at home, eyeing the rain, passing the time with the equivalent of bee chess or poker while the queen glowers because of the "down time," as is said of idle printing presses?

✣

I come late in life to a true relishing of the essays of Montaigne, for his humility and breadth, his genial spirit and lack of absolutism. When Emerson says, "A foolish consistency is the hobgoblin of little minds," he speaks the language of Montaigne, whom he admired; otherwise, there is hardly a line in Emerson which, had Montaigne written it, would not have been qualified with cautious and humble suspension of final judgment.

I was nourished by the Concordian oracles who so confidently announced the laws of life; now, I should prefer that I had sat oftener, in imagination, in Montaigne's third-floor castle library, gazing out with him through the three bay windows at the sixteenth-century Perigueux countryside, discussing with amusement yet with serious honesty our own shortcomings and those of the times.

I like to think that he'd have offered me a glass of very good

107

wine, mildly confessing that he could not tell me its vintage because he was an expert at nothing, and would say, "I scarcely know the difference between the cabbage and the lettuce in my garden."

Late autumn note: I thought a last leaf was falling, alas, down, over and down; but mark, at the rim of Earth it rolled upward in sunlight and rose, wind current by current, a marvelous apparition more bright than any leaf, up to a tree—no leaf, a butterfly.